8/10

BASICS
DESIGN

08

Gavin Ambrose
Paul Harris

DESIGN
TH!NKING

Ethical: aware-
ness/
reflect-
ion/
debate

ava
academia

An AVA Book
Published by AVA Publishing SA
Rue des Fontenailles 16
Case Postale
1000 Lausanne 6
Switzerland
Tel: +41 786 005 109
Email: enquiries@avabooks.ch

Distributed by Thames & Hudson (ex-North America)
181a High Holborn
London WC1V 7QX
United Kingdom
Tel: +44 20 7845 5000
Fax: +44 20 7845 5055
Email: sales@thameshudson.co.uk
www.thamesandhudson.com

Distributed in the USA & Canada by:
Ingram Publisher Services Inc.
1 Ingram Blvd.
La Vergne TN 37086
USA
Tel: +1 866 400 5351
Fax: +1 800 838 1149
Email: customer.service@ingrampublisherservices.com

English Language Support Office
AVA Publishing (UK) Ltd.
Tel: +44 1903 204 455
Email: enquiries@avabooks.ch

ISBN 978-2-940411-17-7

10 9 8 7 6 5 4 3 2 1

Design and text by Gavin Ambrose and Paul Harris
Original photography by Xavier Young
www.xavieryoung.co.uk

Production by AVA Book Production Pte. Ltd., Singapore
Tel: +65 6334 8173
Fax: +65 6259 9830
Email: production@avabooks.com.sg

Design Thinking

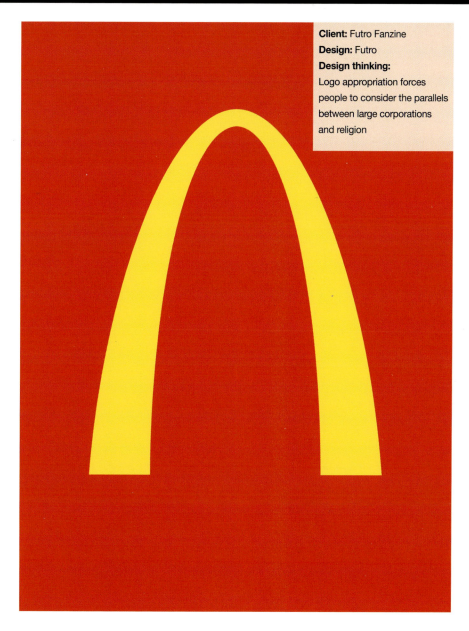

Client: Futro Fanzine
Design: Futro
Design thinking:
Logo appropriation forces people to consider the parallels between large corporations and religion

Futro Fanzine

This poster, created by Futro, appropriates a famous fast-food logo and adapts it to the context of organised religion by making it appear like a church building or bishop's mitre. The appropriation transfers the fast-food brand characteristics and colour scheme to the new context and implies that organised religion is akin to a massive global brand with great marketing muscle. The design questions how people view both large corporations and religion.

Design thinking

Contents

Frost Design

NB Studio

Studio Myerscough

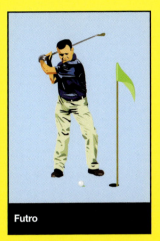

Futro

Studio Output

Peter and Paul

Introduction

'You cannot hold a design in your hand. It is not a thing. It is a process. A system. A way of thinking.'
Bob Gill, *Graphic Design as a Second Language*

Design is an iterative process and design thinking is present in each stage of the journey from client brief to finished work. Different solutions can be produced for any given brief and these can differ widely in levels of creativity, practicality and budget.

This book aims to present an overview of the design thinking involved at each stage of the design process: the methods used by designers to generate and refine creative ideas, the key considerations that help shape them and the feedback and review elements that allow design teams to learn from each job and contribute to future commissions.

Through detailed studies of contemporary work and analysis of the basic theories, we examine how a designer can generate and resolve ideas to produce creative solutions that best meet the stated aims of a brief.

Stages of thinking

An overview of the different stages of the design process and the key considerations of each stage to produce a successful design, with a focus on the design brief and project definition stage.

Research

This section looks at the stage at which information is collected to help generate design ideas. This includes consumer profiles and target group definitions, quantitative and qualitative information and feedback from past projects.

Idea generation

Here we look at how designers use different methods and sources of inspiration to generate creative solutions to the brief. These include sketching, brainstorming and the different paradigms used through design history.

Refinement

This section looks at how a general design concept can be refined. We will examine how images, words, colour and substrates can be used to enhance the idea and increase its effectiveness.

Prototyping

Design ideas need to be presented and articulated to test target group acceptance and receive client approval. Here we see how models, dummies and storyboards can be used to convey ideas so that they can be understood in this context.

Implementation

This section looks at how ideas come to life through production. Implementation must ensure that design details are put into effect and that the client is happy with the final product.

Client: Getty Images
Design: Gavin Ambrose
Design thinking: Choice of photographs to echo the message being conveyed by the design

Getty Images

These cards were created by Gavin Ambrose to announce the upcoming office move for the sports department at Getty Images. The images by Julian Herbert (top) and Mike Hewitt (bottom) depict dramatic movement, reflecting the physical movement of the company's office. The cards also use humour; as one group of animals is running away, the other group is just arriving.

Design thinking Introduction

This book introduces different aspects of design thinking via dedicated chapters for each topic. Each chapter provides numerous examples from leading contemporary design studios, showing unique and creative design thinking and with a detailed analysis to explain the reasons behind the design choices made.

Key design principles are isolated so that the reader can see how they are applied in practice.

Clear navigation

Each chapter has a clear strapline, which allows readers to quickly locate areas of interest.

Introductions

Special section introductions outline basic concepts that will be discussed.

Samples and feedback

46 **47**

Samples and feedback

Understanding the motivations, behaviours and aspirations of a target group often involves detailed study of that group. As it is not possible to quiz every member of the target population, a sample group is typically defined.

Samples

A sample group is typically a collection of five to ten people who share the characteristics of the target group and who can be used for one-to-one interviews, questionnaires and focus groups. The sample should be as representative as possible of the overall population under study and should be selected by first determining the most important attributes that define the group. These may include age, education level, ethnicity and socio-economic group.

Feedback

Design is an iterative process, during which internal and external feedback is sought and received at all stages. The main learning opportunity comes at the end of the process when feedback about the performance, acceptance and success of a design is sought and fed back into the design process. The aim of this is to maintain or improve performance or to better control the process.

Cluster and vote, deciding which ideas to develop

This is a method used to identify patterns in a problem area or in a series of ideas to help the design team select appropriate solutions. This system uses agreed assessment criteria that can take into account the concerns of multiple stakeholders. These criteria are brainstormed, refined, agreed and structured to encourage participants to consider the perspectives of other stakeholders.

Scoring methods

All design ideas are to be scored against the individual selection criteria and then these will be totalled to produce a final score for each idea.

Client: London College of Fashion

Design: Moving Brands

Design thinking: Interactive presentation allows viewers to leave feedback.

London College of Fashion

The Looking Glass, London College of Fashion's 2008 graduate exhibition, showcased the work of 600 students to an industry audience looking for future stars. The ingenious design of the exhibition saw each student represented by a postcard-sized tag which, when placed on a custom-built responsive table, would activate an interactive projection of the student's work on the table surface. The table interface was designed so that the viewer could control whose digital portfolio of work was being shown via these tags. As such, through their choice of tags, the viewer provided explicit feedback about what they wanted to see. The dark monochrome palette and mirroring effects underlined the 'looking glass' theme that was intended to give a sense of transparency and intrigue.

Design Thinking Research

Design Thinking Samples and feedback

Examples

Commercial projects from contemporary studios and designers bring to life the principles under discussion.

Diagrams

Diagrams add meaning to theory by showing the basic principles in action.

Thinking in images

Images have the ability to convey an idea or a lot of information very quickly, which is why images are such a prominent part of graphic design. As we all know, a picture paints a thousand words, so it is worth spending adequate time on image selection and presentation.

Images can be used to communicate in many different ways as they are very versatile and their reading can be conditioned by other factors at play during their presentation. Images can have different cultural and social interpretations and these can be shaped by the contexts within which they are used. The cultural groups they are directed towards, the inclusion or exclusion of particular signs and symbols shared by a cultural group, the use or absence of conditioning agents such as wit and humour and appropriation of historical meaning, are all factors that might influence the meaning drawn from an image. The way an image or design is rendered also has an impact; a black-and-white sketch conveys a different feel from a glossy print, for example.

Receiving and interpreting images
What this means in practice is that one cannot just show a picture of a house. The designer must think about other design aspects that will condition how the viewer receives or interprets the image of the house. Does the house represent an Englishman's castle, a home, an architectural work, a source of joy or sorrow?

Additional information

Clients, designers and the design thinking used are included here.

Captions

Key points are explained within the context of an example project.

Design thinking How to get the most out of this book

Design is a process that turns a brief or requirement into a finished product or design solution. The design process can be said to comprise seven stages: define, research, ideate, prototype, select, implement and learn. Each of these requires design thinking. This chapter will outline each of the seven stages and the design thinking aspects they entail, while subsequent chapters will look at specific stages of the process in more detail.

The design process engages a high degree of creativity but in a way that is controlled and directed by the process so that it is channelled towards producing a viable, practical solution to the design problem, meeting or excelling the stated aims of the brief.

While creativity in design is important, design is an activity that serves economic as well as creative goals. The design process helps ensure that a design satisfies all such considerations. The process seeks to generate a number of possible solutions and utilises various techniques or mechanisms that encourage participants to think outside the box in the pursuit of creative or innovative solutions.

The creative studio (facing page)

These images depict Studio Myerscough's design studio in London, UK. The space facilitates creative thinking and presents an organised chaos, laden with stimuli, and more ordered than it might first appear. The walls are used to thematically collate research and meeting zones are informal, facilitating brainstorming and working space. The space is flexible and adaptable and can be filled and refreshed to help the design thinking process continue its cycle.

The design process

Within the design process, seven steps can be identified: define, research, ideate, prototype, select, implement and learn.

First, the design problem and the target audience needs to be **defined**. A precise understanding of the problem and its constraints allows more exact solutions to be developed. This stage determines what is necessary for the project to be successful. The **research** stage reviews information such as the history of the design problem, end-user research and opinion-led interviews, and identifies potential obstacles.

Ideate is the stage where end-user motivations and needs are identified and ideas are generated to meet these, perhaps through brainstorming.

Prototyping sees the resolve or working-up of these ideas, which are presented for user-group and stakeholder review, prior to being presented to the client.

Selection sees the proposed solutions reviewed against the design brief objective. Some solutions might be practical but may not be the best ones.

Implementation sees design development and its final delivery to the client.

Learning helps designers improve their performance and, for this reason, designers should seek client and target audience feedback and determine if the solution met the goals of the brief. This may identify improvements that can be made in the future.

While the design process is often linear, as shown below, it frequently involves revisiting earlier segments for reworking as it evolves.

Design Thinking Stages of thinking

The seven stages of design

| Define | Research Background | Ideate Solutions | Prototype Resolve | Select Rationale | Implement Delivery | Learn Feedback |

Client: Christie's
Design: Studio AS/
Gavin Ambrose
Design thinking: Unusual
approach to catalogue design,
resulting from research,
prototyping and experience

Christie's

This catalogue was created for an auction of Princess Margaret's (Queen Elizabeth II's younger sister) estate. Photographs of the princess wearing items of jewellery that are to be auctioned are displayed alongside photographs of the pieces themselves. Where possible, the pieces are shown at actual size. This level of detail challenges the norm in catalogue listings and came about as a result of research, prototyping and accumulated experience from producing catalogues.

Design Thinking The design process

Stage 1 – Define
Establishing what the problem is.

This is the first stage in any design process and almost always involves generating or receiving a design brief.

The brief
A design brief presents the client's requirements for a job. These may be verbal or written, simple or complex. A brief contains a specific goal that is to be met by the design but it may also be couched in terms that have varying interpretations.

A brief may be as basic as 'we need a brochure that makes us appeal to 20–30-year-olds' or 'we need a brochure that makes us appear cool and stylish'. As a working relationship develops between a designer and a client over several jobs, a greater understanding of what key terms mean is obtained. A designer needs to interpret the brief and define what words such as 'stylish' and 'cool' mean. This ensures that both parties have shared expectations. This may involve questioning the validity of the brief's elements. For example, a brochure might not be the best way to reach out and appeal to 20–30-year-olds, and perhaps an online campaign would be more effective?

Writing and re-writing a brief
Clients have varying experiences of design services. For this reason, the quality of the briefs that they provide will also vary. A brief needs to include anything that will allow the design team to initiate the design process. However, if it is not robust enough, it may need to be rewritten and reworked with the client.

Checklist:
Do you understand what the client is asking for?

Does the client understand what they are asking for?

Do you agree on the definition of terms?

Does the brief have any flaws?

Can you manage client expectations?

The first stage is to define the problem accurately

Design Thinking Stages of thinking

Define
Brief

Research
Background

Ideate
Solutions

Prototype
Resolve

Select
Rationale

Implement
Delivery

Learn
Feedback

Emótica

This design brief was given to design studio Emotica by Continental Gold, a Colombian gold exploration company. Emotica was asked to produce a new visual identity for use on all the client's external communications.

Aim:

- To produce a new corporate identity that reflects the exciting potential of this junior mining exploration company.

- To create an identity that resonates with potential investors as the company prepares to raise its profile ahead of an IPO.

- To differentiate the company from other mining companies, other gold companies, and other companies on the stock market in general.

Usage: The identity will be used on all external corporate communications including website, printed materials, business cards and presentations.

Geographical locations: The target audience mainly reside in North America and Europe.

Target audience: Shareholders, bank analysts, media and other interested parties.

Identity keys that relate to the nature of the company:

Nouns: Colombia, gold, mining, exploration, Antioquia, history

Adjectives: unique, new, exciting potential, impressive, experienced

Colours: gold, bright forest green, (Colombian flag colours: red, blue, yellow)

Who: the activity the client and target audience is active in.

Why: to create a coherent visual identity/advance aims.

What: a corporate visual identity to attract investors.

Where: on all print and web-based external communications.

Who: to attract new and existing business interest.

Descriptors or keys: nouns, verbs and attributes that can be used to create the unique selling proposition the design presents.

Resulting identity: the words 'gold' and 'Colombia' are picked out to highlight the USP of its business: gold in Colombia. The dark green achieves high contrast and reflects Colombia's climate.

Continental GOLD
The Colombia Play

Objectives
Objectives are simply what the client hopes to achieve through commissioning a design job, and it is important that these are fully understood and 'mapped' to your design thinking.

Objectives need to be specified so that the design team knows what it has to achieve. Asking the client simple questions gets to the heart of the matter and focuses on what the client expects, what the project boundaries are and what deliverables are required.

'The Five Ws' (borrowed from news writing), refers to five words beginning with 'w', which, when asked, elicit factual answers that are necessary to adequately define a design job. They are: who, what, when, where and why ('how' is often tacked on to the end too). Asking questions such as these provides detail that the design team can use throughout the design process and identifies key restraints that they have to work to.

1 **Who** is the client and target audience? (size, nature, characteristics)

2 **What** design solution is the client thinking of? (print, web, video)

3 **When** will the design be needed and for how long? (project timescales)

4 **Where** will the design be used? (media, location, country)

5 **Why** does the client think a design solution is required?

+ **How** will the solution be implemented? (budget, distribution, campaign)

The proposition

Definition of the design brief and its objectives should enable the design team to establish the general proposition of a design. The proposition can be used to describe the general ideas and values that a design intends to present to, and be internalised by, the target audience. Once the proposition has been determined it can be more precisely defined and articulated to the audience.

For example, an electrical manufacturer produces electrical goods, but so do many other companies. This particular manufacturer's values include being reliable and giving quality service. Again, this is not unique. The proposition needs to go beyond simply 'what' someone does. By spending time thinking about the proposition of a design, subsequent design thinking time will be focused and meaningful.

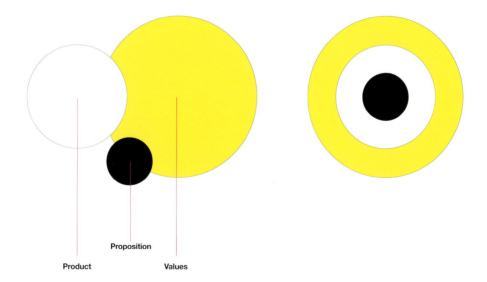

Proposition

Product   Values

The USP, or point of difference

Having a clear understanding of the product, values and the proposition will inform your thinking at each stage of the thinking process, and aligning these three facets will ensure a targeted delivery of an idea.

Stage 2 – Research
Collecting background information.

Once the brief has been defined and agreed, a designer starts to search for information that can be fed into the creative process at the ideate stage. This research can be either quantitative, with hard statistical numbers about the size and composition of target user groups, or qualitative, with information about what that user group buys or consumes and what their lifestyle is like. It may be pertinent to build a mental model of a typical user in order to enable the design team to obtain a good feel for what would appeal to them. This includes factors such as education, career, holiday destinations, musical tastes, aspirations and so on.

Primary research
A primary source of research is the feedback generated during the learning phase of projects previously undertaken with the same or similar clients. Such feedback provides a starting point with regard to what worked and what did not work with a specific target group.

Secondary research
Secondary research is the information obtained from general secondary sources such as consumer market research reports. These provide the demographic breakdown and historic performance of given markets and market segments, and provide a clear view of how a market is structured.

Checklist
Do you have feedback from previous projects?

Do you have a statistical composition of the user group?

Do you understand the target market?

What is the education level of the user group?

What is the typical lifestyle of the user group?

What are the aspirations of the user group?

Design Thinking Stages of thinking

The second stage sees a period of research

Define
Brief

Research
Background

Ideate
Solutions

Prototype
Resolve

Select
Rationale

Implement
Delivery

Learn
Feedback

deas boards

These ideas boards were compiled by design studio The Team, for four different projects. Competitor nformation and references from other sectors and markets are collated, together with material from reference books and magazines, to give a broad background of the projects' 'topographies' or andscapes. All of this information will be fed back into the design process at the ideate stage.

Stage 3 – Ideate
Creating potential solutions.

During the ideate stage, the design team draws on the research gathered and the constraints established during the define stage. This information is used to create ideas with which to tackle the design brief.

Designers use different methods to ideate, some of which will be discussed in more detail in chapter 3, 'Idea generation'. Ideation methods include brainstorming, sketching ideas, adapting a tried-and-tested design that already exists, taking a top-down analytical approach that focuses on the product, service or company or a bottom-up approach that focuses on the customer or user (both are further explained on page 56). Each method involves a varying degree of creativity and choosing which method to use will depend on factors such as how much money is available and how original the design needs to be.

At this stage, a design team might also choose to harness one of the multitude of art and design movements or paradigms. A design brief can be given a modernist, abstract, constructivist or a deconstructivist interpretation, for example.

As the ideate stage progresses, it will become clear whether there are any misunderstandings or shortcomings in the definition stage and whether sufficient levels of research were carried out. Feedback can be sought throughout the design process to clarify points of doubt with the client and to address aspects that were ill-defined during the definition stage.

Checklist:
Do you understand the brief?

Do you have sufficient research information?

Which methods will be used for idea generation?

Design Thinking Stages of thinking

During the ideate stage, design ideas are developed

Define
Brief

Research
Background

**Ideate
Solutions**

Prototype
Resolve

Select
Rationale

Implement
Delivery

Learn
Feedback

ANISH KAPOOR

Client: Barbican Art Gallery
Design: Research Studios
Design thinking: Ideas for an initial design concept generated through visual brainstorming

K A N I S H R A P O O R

ANISH KAPOOR

Barbican Art Gallery

These are some of the initial design concepts generated by Research Studios for an Anish Kapoor show at the Barbican in London. Time has been spent experimenting or visually brainstorming, setting the artist's name in various typefaces to create different visual statements. This experimental time can prove invaluable, allowing your mind to wander, and your hand to 'doodle'. This period allows for experimentation, without considering what is 'right' or 'wrong', rejecting preconceptions in favour of free-thinking.

Stage 4 – Prototype
Resolving solutions.

The ideate stage generates a variety of potential solutions to the design brief. Prior to selection, it may be necessary to further work up the most promising of these solutions. This will allow particular aspects to be tested and will provide a better basis for comparison at the selection stage. In such cases a prototype can be created.

A prototype can be used to test the technical feasibility of a design idea to see if it works as a physical object. Novel packaging or presentation ideas normally require the development of a prototype. A prototype can also test the visual aspects of the design by presenting them as they would be produced. This also provides the opportunity to test, where pertinent, a design in three dimensions.

A prototype gives the design team and client the ability to visualise and handle a design concept, to get an idea of its physical presence and tactile qualities.

As a prototype aims to test particular aspects of a design solution, it must be made so that those aspects are present and can be effectively evaluated. To convey the idea of what it will look like, a prototype does not need to be made with the final materials. For example, architectural models are often made from whiteboard and aim to give a three-dimensional visualisation of a building design. However, if a particular print finish is stipulated, it may be pertinent to present this via a prototype.

Checklist:
Do all potential solutions require prototyping?

What elements will the prototype test?

What functionality will the prototype have?

Design Thinking Stages of thinking

Prototyping designs adds detail and resolution, and allows for testing

Define
Brief

Research
Background

Ideate
Solutions

Prototype
Resolve

Select
Rationale

Implement
Delivery

Learn
Feedback

Client: Henk Hubenet
Design: Faydherbe/de Vringer
Design thinking: Images form a visual model of the proposed solution, prior to construction

Henk Hubenet

Faydherbe/de Vringer were asked by Henk Hubenet to create an installation for a project called Ruimtevaart, which seeks to acquire workspace for artists as part of a visual arts project. The proposed installation design features a multitude of images that form a visual model, creating an impression of what the workspace will look like once it has been built.

Design Thinking Stage 4 – Prototype

Stage 5 – Select
Making choices.

The select stage is the point at which one of the proposed design solutions is chosen for development. The key decision criterion is fitness for purpose: does the design meet the needs and goals of the brief, and will it effectively communicate to the target audience to achieve those aims? The winning design is typically that which most closely meets the design brief, or a significant part of it. It may not be possible or desirable to meet all the requirements of a brief within a single design. For example, market segmentation increasingly calls for different marketing and design solutions for different segments.

Other factors, such as cost and time, are relevant in the selection process, but these may change as the process develops. The budget available may not provide for the preferred solution and so a more humble option may be selected. However, budget and time constraints should be identified during the definition stage and must be considered throughout the design process.

A studio may advance what it thinks are the best design solutions to the client, and while its opinion and advice are important, the client knows its business, market and clients best and will make the final choice. This could well be different to the designer's preferred choice. At the end of the selection process, the client will sign off the choice, thus initiating the next stage in the design process.

Checklist:
Does the design meet the defined needs of the brief?
Does the design resonate with the target audience?
Can the design be produced on time and on budget?
Are there other factors to take into account?
Has the client signed off the design?

Design Thinking Stages of thinking

The select stage allows only possible designs to be fully developed

| Define | Research | Ideate | Prototype | Select | Implement | Learn |
| Brief | Background | Solutions | Resolve | Rationale | Delivery | Feedback |

Progress boards

Pictured is a progress board created by The Team as part of a commission for The King's Fund, a UK healthcare charity. Notice how it shows different design elements such as typefaces, colours and positionals to give an approximation of what a final design may look like. A design team may have to work up an idea in considerable detail before it can decide which idea is best.

Stage 6 – Implement

Delivering the solution to the design brief.

During this stage, the designer passes the design artwork and format specifications to those who will be supplying the final product. This might be a printer, web builder or fabricator. This moment provides a good opportunity to confirm the production specifications such as print quantity and what you expect to receive. For example, a printer is usually given some leeway to account for set-up in the different steps of the the print process. This means an order for 100 flyers may not result in the receipt of 100. It may be more or may be less. By double-checking, everyone is clear about the level of expectation, and what the client expectations are.

The design team typically provides project management during this stage, in order to ensure that the end results meet design expectations, and to keep the project on budget and on time. Proofing may be necessary during implementation if a print job is involved. This will ensure that what is printed is an accurate reflection of the artwork supplied. For websites and other electronic media, proofing means testing functionality as well as the visual appearance. This stage ends with the final delivery to the client of the finished job.

Checklist:

Has the client signed off the designs?

Have printers or other production professionals been booked?

Has the artwork been delivered to production professionals?

Has the job been proofed against the design?

Has the finished job been delivered?

Design Thinking Stages of thinking

The implement stage of the design process sees the design put into production

Define Brief — **Research** Background — **Ideate** Solutions — **Prototype** Resolve — **Select** Rationale — **Implement** Delivery → **Learn** Feedback

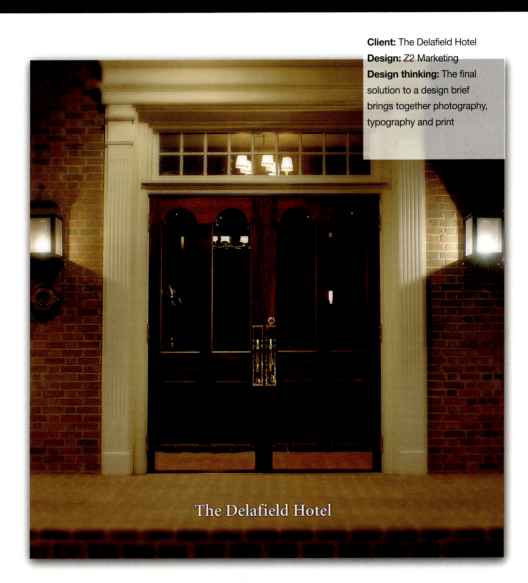

Client: The Delafield Hotel
Design: Z2 Marketing
Design thinking: The final solution to a design brief brings together photography, typography and print

The Delafield Hotel

The Delafield Hotel

This brochure cover features an image of the doors to the establishment; a simple but deceptively clever visual metaphor for a welcome. The production of the brochure is the culmination of the design process and brings together photography, typography, copywriting, design and print in a final product.

Design Thinking Stage 6 – Implement

Stage 7 – Learn
Obtaining feedback.

The final stage in the process involves learning from what has happened throughout the design process. This is a feedback stage during which the client and design agency might seek to identify what worked well and where there is room for improvement.

Following the implementation, the client may begin to look for or receive feedback on how the product has been received by the target audience and how beneficial its effects on the target audience have been. Thus, a design firm can find out how the audience responded to the design.

The feedback generated at the end of the process becomes a learning opportunity for future projects. It forms one of the sources of information for the define and research stages. Any problems with the design may have been because of inadequacies in the brief or lack of understanding of key points. Through the feedback process, designers and clients build up a shared understanding over time. This serves to facilitate the production of increasingly optimal solutions in the future.

Although the learn stage appears to be the last of the seven that we've identified, it actually occurs throughout the design process. At each stage you should take stock of where you are, where you are heading, what's working and what's not. The ability to learn from each stage will enhance the development of design thinking, and will help to generate radical and successful designs.

Checklist:
Has dialogue with the client about the success of implementation taken place?
How successful was the implementation?
What feedback has the client received or commissioned?
What aspects can be improved?

Design Thinking Stages of thinking

The learn stage is a valuable chance to refine and learn from the design thinking process

Define
Brief

Research
Background

Ideate
Solutions

Prototype
Resolve

Select
Rationale

Implement
Delivery

Learn
Feedback

Client: Australian
Directors Guild
Design: Frost Design
Design thinking: Client
feedback used to inform
a new design direction

katherine giovenali
event manager
events@adg.org.au

australian
directors
guild

PO Box 211
Rozelle NSW
Australia 2039
PH: +61 2 9555 7045
FAX: +61 2 9555 7086
AH: +61 2 9990 6702
www.adg.org.au

Australian Directors Guild

Frost Design was asked by the Australian Directors Guild to redesign their
logo. The starting point for the new logo design was feedback from the client:
its existing logo was old and no longer represented its aims or those of its
members. The new logo uses the association's initial letterforms to represent
a camera aperture. This is overlayed on portraits of the directors in such a
way that it represents the interplay between the eye of the director and that
of the camera.

Design Thinking Stage 7 – Learn

These pages show the various different stages of the design process within the context of an actual design job. The sequence shows the design thinking at each step of the process.

Stage 1 – Define

Sovereign is the parent organisation to a number of housing associations in England and as such, over time, has acquired a number of identities and brands. Design studio The Team was tasked with creating a new visual identity to bring all the different aspects of Sovereign's business under one overall umbrella design. The Team's brief was to create a strong brand identity using the Sovereign name. This would then need to be paired with a description to clearly identify the sub-brand, and would require a unique idea at its core in order to help the associations stand out from their competitors.

Stage 2 – Research

The Team undertook research to find out what made Sovereign different from other housing associations. This research included interviews and workshops with the client and consultation with the regional associations it had acquired in order to get a feel for the values and vision they had for the brand. An audit of competitors was undertaken to better understand the visual world that housing associations work in. The research showed that many felt that Sovereign's ability to balance the needs of current customers, while planning and developing for future customers, was its strongest asset. A web-based search for imagery and icons to represent the concepts of continuity and growth was also carried out to help generate ideas for the visual stimulus for the identity.

Research included a web-based search for images using a circle or loop, representing continuity and growth. This would form the central part of the visual identity.

The design team made a series of initial sketches (above) exploring and developing ideas for a symbol. Different symbol ideas were worked up and given different treatments to develop and test them (right).

Stage 3 – Ideate

The initial ideas of the design team had the central concept of planning for today as well as tomorrow. The team wanted to create a shape or expression that could be used for the group logo as well as all its sub-brands. Initial sketches looked to create an abstract shape to represent the core idea of continuity and growth, which could be used to create larger graphics or expressions across printed materials to support the logo and brand concept. The initial ideas that went forward all carried a strong sense of this and appeared intricate and made up of many parts or sides. This helped reflect the different elements and areas of the client's business.

Design Thinking Example project

Stage 4 – Select

Three different design ideas were advanced to the select stage. The first was a Möbius strip idea, rendered in a 3D form to give a dynamic, sculptural and organic feel. There are many possible permutations for this logo shape, but the more angular shape used adds a feeling of energy and movement. The second route evolved from a two-sided yin-yang balance into a constantly moving and intertwined form. The third unites two interdependent shapes with a feeling of continuity and strength. These ideas were presented to the client on boards to facilitate discussion of each option.

Presentations of the three design ideas for selection.

Stage 5 – Prototype

The chosen design was refined using different treatments. The symbol is derived from a Möbius strip (a surface with only one side and only one boundary component), a never-ending shape that flows back into itself as its contours are followed by the eye. This reflects the relationship between addressing the changing needs of current customers while planning and developing to satisfy those of tomorrow. The sculptural and contoured form gives a feeling of strength and stability while the fluid triangular shape and dynamic, translucent shading captures an energetic and forward-looking spirit that is reinforced by the orange colour. The symbol is complemented by an uncomplicated yet powerful logotype that provides a strong and balanced relationship between the two elements. Lowercase lettering creates a professional, streamlined appearance.

Different forms of the resolved logo.

Stage 6 – Implement
The final design was rolled out across Sovereign's brands and sub-brands.
This included all printed materials, such as stationery, ID cards, report covers,
brochures and newsletters, as well as signage for vehicle livery and clothing.
The logo also featured on signage around its corporate and local offices, as well
as on building sites where Sovereign works to develop land and build new homes.

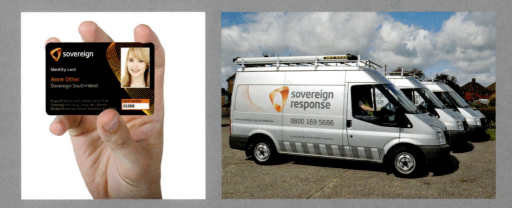

The final design was rolled out across Sovereign's brands and sub-brands.

Stage 7 – Learn
Learning occurred throughout the design process. The select process gave
the design team a clear idea of what solutions resonated with the client, while
client feedback following implementation would indicate which aspects were
well received by its customers and which were not.

Design Thinking Example project

Client: BOAI
Design: unthink
Design thinking: Product usage identified and incorporated in design

Research

Once a brief has been defined and agreed the research stage can begin. The research stage is when the design team investigates the subject matter of the brief in order to accumulate relevant information that will be used to inform design decisions.

Various data gathering methods exist to generate quantitative and qualitative information. This information will, in turn, provide different ways of identifying, determining and dissecting the attitudes and behaviours of the target audience. It will also help to provide an understanding of the design approach taken by competing products, brands and organisations.

Research into the target group is necessary in order for the design to contain the information hooks or drivers required for effective communication with that group. It also enables the design to avoid containing information hooks or drivers that might alienate or disenfranchise the target group.

Obtaining a clear understanding of the target audience feeds information into the ideate stage. This is then used to generate ideas for a design solution.

This section outlines some of the research techniques that design teams use to obtain a better understanding of the business of the client and the composition of the target group.

BOAI (facing page)

This DVD features a double-take image of someone holding a DVD. A DVD is a finite shape and a relatively small 'canvas' on which to place a design, but use of applied design thinking means that it is always possible to generate a creative solution. At a basic level this design shows the product being used, an aspect that the design team often seeks to identify during the research process. The target audience appreciated the irony and sense of humour of this design.

Identifying drivers

The research stage aims to identify the drivers that stimulate the target group to act on a design and the barriers that could impede the success of a design.

Drivers

Drivers are the knowledge and conditions that initiate and support activities for which the design was created. Knowledge and conditions can include such terms of reference as market forces, fashions and musical trends of the day.

By identifying these drivers, the design team will have an appreciation of the stimuli that people are receptive to. For example, market forces in the newspaper sector are moving towards online publication and away from print publication. Someone intending to launch a new communication product would need to be aware of such a driver.

Barriers

Barriers need to be identified during the research stage in order to prevent work from being undertaken in a direction that has little chance of being implemented for technical, legal or market reasons. Barriers can be rules and laws about what product packaging can and cannot show, for example. Technical barriers might include systems of standards that exist in different countries. The size of envelopes that postal companies prefer to use, for example, might affect the format of mass mailers. Market barriers include the purchasing and distribution power of key competitors, is something that might restrict access to outlets.

Drivers can also act as barriers. By not following the driver, for example, the designer could be creating an obstacle that reduces the chance of success for a design. For example, launching a new newspaper at a time when consumers are moving to online content sources appears to be counter-intuitive.

Design Thinking Research

Stimulation

The action of agents (stimuli) on our physical or emotional condition. The presence of stimuli produces a response; for example, participation in adventure sports may produce the response of a feeling of exhilaration or elation.

Client: What 2 Do
Design: Faydherbe/de Vringer
Design thinking: Logo design showing identification and acknowledgement of some of the barriers faced by the target audience

what2do
loopbaanbegeleiding
en coaching

Viviënstraat 90
2582 RW Den Haag

... with your career?
... with your life?
... with your personal development?
... when emotions are too strong?
... with conflicts?
... when you want to develop your people into professionals?
... when your team doesn't cooperate?

www.what2dowith.eu

what2do
is lid van NOLOC
vereniging voor loopbaan
professionals

what2do
loopbaanbegeleiding
en coaching

Freya van Hemert tot Dingshof

Viviënstraat 90
2582 RW Den Haag

T   06 51 93 98 83
E   info@what2dowith.eu
W   www.what2dowith.eu

What 2 Do

These stationery elements form part of an identity created by Faydherbe/de Vringer for a career accompaniment and training organisation, What 2 Do. What 2 Do aims to encourage people to step towards different potential careers. By incorporating the question, 'What to do?', the logo design acknowledges the barriers that its clients will need to overcome. A visual representation in the shape of an arrow shows the way. By outlining a direction, the logo becomes a driver for action.

Information gathering

When conducting research, information can be classified into two categories: quantitative and qualitative. These help define the size of a target market and its characteristics.

Quantitative

Quantitative information is numerical or statistical information that enables a design team to put physical dimensions to a target market. Total market sales value, annual sales volume and the number of consumers in the 25–30-year-old age group are all examples of quantitative information.

Qualitative

Qualitative information allows the design team to understand why things are as they are; the reasons that people respond to certain stimuli or not. Qualitative information is typically obtained via face-to-face interviews where participants talk about their experience and preferences for a given topic. This is usually undertaken via a group discussion or focus group, or an in-depth interview with carefully selected individuals.

Types of survey

Qualitative and quantitative information can be obtained from reference libraries, but if the information required is not available, different surveys can be commissioned to obtain it. These might include:

Statistical surveys – these collect quantitative information from numerical data

Sampling – this collects information from a population sample in order to represent the whole

Opinion polls – these assess public opinion using sampling

Quantitative market research – this collects data for marketing purposes

Paid statistical surveys – these reward participants for providing information about consumption habits

Questionnaires – these contain a set of questions

Omnibus surveys – these ask questions in a regular shared monthly survey

Client: INSEAD
Design: NB: Studio
Design thinking: Leaf metaphor for information gathering

INSEAD

Pictured is a graphic identity created by NB: Studio for the INSEAD Leadership Summit Asia 2009. To highlight the aims of the summit – to discover new emerging business models – the design features a map of the world formed of leaves. In this way, the design suggests a link between gathering information from around the world and gathering leaves.

Design Thinking Information gathering

Diagram techniques

Diagrams can provide an excellent means of organising the relationships between different pieces of information and ideas. By creating diagrams, a design team can quickly obtain an understanding of how a target group is structured and what some of the key relationships within that group may be. Diagrams also provide a means to help communicate the results of the research stage. They might be used, for example, to present the design team's understanding of the composition of the market to the client.

Various diagrammatic methods can be used to express the different kinds of relationships that will inform the ideate stage. These include sample scatter plots (opposite above) and Venn diagrams (opposite below).

Venn diagrams are a common diagrammatic technique for presenting information about a group. Venn diagrams were created by John Venn in 1880 to show the logical relations between a defined group of sets. The entire population of each set is represented by a circle and the relationship between sets, and the populations they contain, is shown by how the circles interact or overlap with each other.

These interactions show all the possible logical relations between the sets and allow the viewer to visualise the relationships between them. For example, the entire population of men is a subset of the entire population of humans. Pictured here are basic two-set Venn diagrams, showing various relationships between two finite groups.

Using diagrams

Diagrams are used to show the results of quantitative or qualitative information in a readily accessible, visual way to aid comprehension and understanding. A range of different diagrams with increasing levels of complexity have been developed to be able to present detailed information in such a way that key trends or elements of interest can be identified. The diagrammatic methods used need to be appropriate for the data set under investigation and several methods that present other related data are often used in order to construct a model of the subject being analysed.

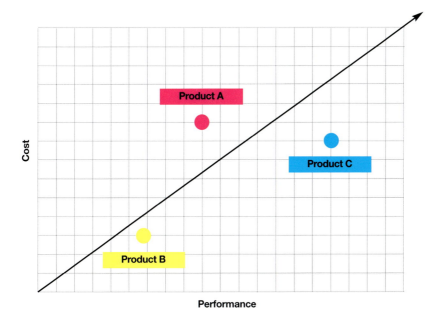

Cost

Performance

A sample scatter plot

Any two or more criteria can be plotted on a scatter plot. This can help the reader to draw meaning from the relationship between the variables. Within design these can be used to articulate to a client where you perceive their product or service to be in relation to others.

Venn diagrams

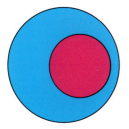

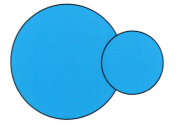

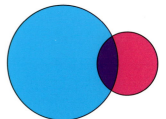

Inclusion

The large circle could be 'humans' and the small circle 'women'. Thus 'women' is a subset of 'human'.

Union

A union is everything in both circles. For example, the population could be sexes that watch TV, with the larger circle being 'men' and the smaller circle being 'women'.

Intersection

The large circle could be 'women' and the small circle 'people who play football'. The shaded area where the two circles overlap represents 'women who play football'.

Design Thinking Information gathering

Target groups

The research stage identifies and provides rudimentary classification to the different groups of consumers or users in a sector and their characteristics.

Once target groups have been identified, they can be further researched to acquire a greater level of detail about their composition and habits, providing both qualitative and quantitative information. For example, the sex, education and income level profile (quantitative information) and the motivations, likes, dislikes and aspirations (qualitative information) of the groups.

This may involve putting oneself in scenarios typical of that group and recording thoughts and observations. Other effects can also be used to simulate the experiences of younger or older users or users with disabilities.

Detailed research allows the design team to construct a target user profile and create a fictional 'typical user' to add colour to the profile. This provides a basis for creating design solutions at the ideate stage.

Checklist:

What are the sex, age and socio-economic demographics for the group?

What education and income level do they have?

What are the lifestyle aspirations of the group?

What media do they buy/consume?

Where do they shop, eat out and take holidays?

Royal Mail (facing page)

Pictured is a presentation pack for an issue of stamps celebrating British cinema. Due to recent closures of many Post Offices in the UK, the new packaging was designed to help expand the market for commemorative stamps. The pack redesign separates the stamps from the pack, thus facilitating their sale in supermarkets and other retail outlets (such collections would traditionally only have been available at Post Office branches). The stamps feature original poster artwork from films such as the *Carry On* and *Hammer House of Horror* series. These required text to be redrawn at small scale as simply reducing a large poster to stamp size would result in the text filling in.

Design Thinking Research

Client: Royal Mail
Design: Webb & Webb
Design thinking: New packaging allows the product to be sold to a wider audience

Character profiles
A character profile is a tool developed during the research stage, containing written and graphic information about a particular group of people. It is used in the design process to stimulate idea formation and help with decision making.

A character profile is built by looking for key words and characteristics that define the target group. These can then be augmented with visual clues such as magazine cuttings and may be used to construct an image of the life led by a fictional representative character of the group. This might include the cars they drive, where they take holidays, the technology they use, their aspirations and any peculiarities. This is a mental model construction, put together through research of the group's habits and buying patterns, brainstorming and other processes to identify and define the key characteristics of the group. Remembering that it is dangerous to make assumptions, character profiles should also be made for the outliers of the group; the more extreme people that may not exhibit typical behaviour, yet share many of the same qualities.

By keeping these storyboards in view while working, a designer has a continual point of reference and the ability to repeatedly ask, 'What would x think of this?' at decision points.

Secondary research
Secondary research sees the collection and use of existing published information about customers, competitors and relevant trends of interest such as social and economic trends. Secondary research can be used to feed general information about the target group, the market and underlying trends into the design process.

Resources
Various secondary data resources are available at public reference libraries and online. These may allow you to automatically repeat a search every day or to subscribe to web feeds. Secondary data sources include newspapers and trade periodicals, blogs, conference papers, market research reports, trade association and official statistics, commercial business reports (KeyNote, Euromonitor, Mintel, Datamonitor and EIU), university research papers and think tanks.

Checklist:
Do we have information at hand to build a character profile?

What key information do we lack?

Do surveys and opinion polls exist that can fill these gaps?

Client: Cadbury
Design: Studio Output
Design thinking: A product relaunch based on the original profile creates a nostalgic buzz and answers the target audience's demands

Cadbury

This campaign was created by Studio Output for the relaunch of the Wispa chocolate bar. The relaunch was in response to public demand for the return of a classic brand. The design was built on the existing character profile and thus created a nostalgic buzz around the brand.

Samples and feedback

Understanding the motivations, behaviours and aspirations of a target group often involves detailed study of that group. As it is not possible to quiz every member of the target population, a sample group is typically defined.

Samples

A sample group is typically a collection of five to ten people who share the characteristics of the target group and who can be used for one-to-one interviews, questionnaires and focus groups. The sample should be as representative as possible of the overall population under study and should be selected by first determining the most important attributes that define the group. These may include age, education level, ethnicity and socio-economic group.

Feedback

Design is an iterative process, during which internal and external feedback is sought and received at all stages. The main learning opportunity comes at the end of the process when feedback about the performance, acceptance and success of a design is sought and fed back into the design process. The aim of this is to maintain or improve performance or to better control the process.

Cluster and vote, deciding which ideas to develop

This is a method used to identify patterns in a problem area or in a series of ideas to help the design team select appropriate solutions. This system uses agreed assessment criteria that can take into account the concerns of multiple stakeholders. These criteria are brainstormed, refined, agreed and structured to encourage participants to consider the perspectives of other stakeholders.

Scoring methods

All design ideas are to be scored against the individual selection criteria and then these will be totalled to produce a final score for each idea.

Client: London College of Fashion
Design: Moving Brands
Design thinking: Interactive presentation allows viewers to leave feedback

London College of Fashion

The Looking Glass, London College of Fashion's 2008 graduate exhibition, showcased the work of 600 students to an industry audience looking for future stars. The ingenious design of the exhibition saw each student represented by a postcard-sized tag which, when placed on a custom-built responsive table, would activate an interactive projection of the student's work on the table surface. The table interface was designed so that the viewer could control whose digital portfolio of work was being shown via these tags. As such, through their choice of tags, the viewer provided explicit feedback about what they wanted to see. The dark monochrome palette and mirroring effects underlined the 'looking glass' theme that was intended to give a sense of transparency and intrigue.

Design Thinking Samples and feedback

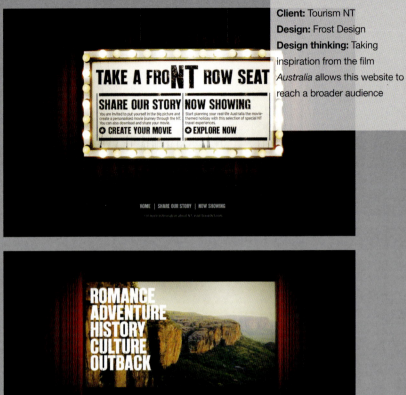

Client: Tourism NT
Design: Frost Design
Design thinking: Taking inspiration from the film *Australia* allows this website to reach a broader audience

Idea generation

Once a design brief has been defined and researched, the idea generation or ideate stage sees concepts created that may solve the design problem. This is the part of the design process where creativity is unleashed. Ideation seeks to generate concepts that will be worked up and resolved in subsequent process stages, and therefore concerns ideas rather than the vocabulary of the design.

Creativity conveys a sense of pure inventiveness and knowing no bounds, yet graphic design requires applied creativity directed towards a specific end. This is informed or controlled by the requirements of the design brief and the qualitative and quantitative information produced during the research stage.

Despite channelling the creative effort in this way, the scope for inventiveness and novelty is not diminished. Design ideas can be generated using various methods and reference points that allow creativity to flourish and produce results in a consistent way as part of an economic activity. This chapter will introduce some of the methods and techniques that designers use to generate design ideas.

Tourism NT (facing page)
This microsite was created to help promote tourism to Australia's Northern Territory. Inspired by Baz Luhrmann's film, *Australia*, set in the Northern Territory, the design solution features a cinema advert (top), other cinema collateral and an interactive microsite to promote destinations within the territory using the themes of the movie (middle). Site visitors enter their name (bottom) and then a one-minute movie is shown starring the various Northern Territory destinations. Promoting the destination in this way provided the client with an opportunity to reach a broader audience.

Basic design directions

Starting from a given point (often the design of existing or competing products, brands or organisations), designers can think in specific 'directions' in order to generate new ideas from existing designs.

Divergence
Divergence is the expansion or spreading out of something from a central point or theme. This can be clearly seen in fields as diverse as market segmentation and typography. Divergence occurs as both an instigator and a response to divergence in society at large as designers respond to changing demographics, and the increasingly diverse market segmentations of their clients.

Convergence
Convergence is the contraction of something towards a central, more generalised point. In design, although the overriding tendency is towards divergence, convergence can still be found in areas such as generic branding. Brands nowadays often take products back to a more basic state or pre-branding time – when a tin of tomatoes was just a tin of tomatoes, for example.

Transformation
Transformation involves a substantial qualitative change, such as the redesign of a visual identity, or a repackage in order to facilitate a new distribution method.

Design Thinking Idea generation

Divergence
Moving away in different directions from a common point. Also called branching out.

Convergence
The coming together of two or more entities towards a central point or common ground.

Transformation
A qualitative change in appearance or character.

Client: Ian Macleod Distillers
Design: Navyblue
Design thinking: A divergence from the typical tradition- and heritage-based approach creates an exciting and unique alternative

Design Thinking Basic design directions

Ian Macleod Distillers

In its redesign of the packaging for Ian Macleod Distillers' Smokehead Scotch whisky, Navyblue took a divergent approach. Using the traditional approach to branding for Scotch whisky as a starting point, Navyblue branched out to create an unusual and unique design. Thus, instead of taking a history- and tradition-based approach to the packaging, it produced a young and energetic image, focusing on the inherent qualities and flavours found within the product.

Once the overall design direction has been chosen, the design team needs to think about how this will relate to the design direction of competing products, brands and organisations. Will the design solution be different or similar, will it stand out or blend in with competitors?

Point of difference or unique selling point (USP)

The point of difference or unique selling point (USP) is the combination of values and attributes that differentiates a company or product from all other similar companies or products. As such, it is a form of divergence as it involves moving away from the designs used by similar companies or brands.

Clustering

Clustering can be found in any town. For example, the presence of many restaurants in one area draws people to that area to eat, although they may not know which restaurant they'll be eating at until they get there. Designs can be created to blend in (converge) with the visual image presented by others in the peer group or can be created to stand out (diverge) from them.

Inclusive design

Inclusive design aims to increase social equality and ensure that products, services and environments are accessible to all people. Given the estimations of some research that by 2020 half the UK adult population will be aged over 50, while 20 per cent of Americans and 25 per cent of Japanese will be over 65, this is becoming an increasingly important factor for consideration.

MTV (facing page)

Pictured here are two MySpace web pages created for MTV. Both feature transformation in content delivery and content presentation. The page on the left is taken from the new MTV UK MySpace site, developed so that the MySpace Chart Application could be shared over the MySpace network while allowing MTV to share exclusive content with its users. The MySpace page pulls content from the MTV UK website, which makes publishing content easier. This is a cluster design as its general presentation structure is similar to that commonly found on web pages.

The page on the right is taken from MTV's FUR TV MySpace site. Here, the design has moved away from the typical MySpace layout to make the pages look like a desk or bulletin board. This design is inclusive as it has a familiar, engaging look with snippets of information that are easy to locate. The level of detail on a typical website, on the other hand, may act as a barrier to older people or to those who are more receptive to visual presentation of information.

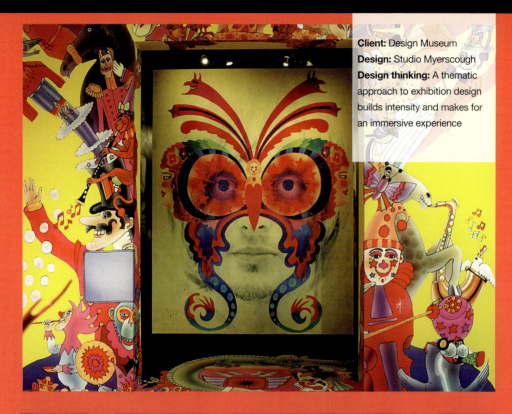

Client: Design Museum
Design: Studio Myerscough
Design thinking: A thematic approach to exhibition design builds intensity and makes for an immersive experience

Design Thinking Idea generation

Client: Crawley Library
Design: Gordon Young and Why Not Associates
Design thinking: Sand-blasted typography transforms, yet converges, diverse texts

Crawley Library

These typographic tree sculptures are an example of transformation and convergence. The design features 14 trees, installed throughout the library building from floor to ceiling like supporting pillars. Sand-blasted into the trunks are extracts from literature, typographically executed to reflect the diverse subject matter of the texts held within the library.

Design Museum (facing page)

These rooms were created by Studio Myerscough for an exhibition about the British designer Alan Aldridge at London's Design Museum. The design concentrates on the fantasy aspect of Aldridge's work with an intensity that makes the exhibition immersive, all-consuming and that delivers a sense of theatre.

Design Thinking Basic design directions

Themes of thinking

Designers often have to face the challenge of fitting large quantities of information into formats with limited space. Several tenets can be used to inform the design process and help overcome this challenge.

KISS

Keep It Short and Simple, or Keep It Simple Stupid (KISS) is a modern acronym but it employs the same tenets as Ockham's razor, which has been around for several hundred years. The idea is to pare back a design to its essential elements, something that requires a clear understanding of the message that has to be communicated and the audience it is to be directed towards.

Focus

Select only the key message elements as the focus for the design. A company may have many products or projects but the design should focus on the most important ones. Information about other aspects of the company can be provided via other communications such as printed materials, brochures or the web page.

Top down and bottom up

An analytical approach appropriated from information technology development, this looks at a design problem from the system perspective and then 'drills' down to add detail in specific areas (top down), or focuses on the basic elements first and works upwards to link these together as part of a system (bottom up).

Ockham's razor

Ockham's razor is a principle attributed to the fourteenth-century English logician and Franciscan friar, William of Ockham, and it forms the basis of methodological reductionism. The principle states that elements that are not really needed should be pared back to produce something simpler and in doing so, the risk of introducing inconsistencies, ambiguities and redundancies will be reduced. Ockham's razor is also referred to as the principle of parsimony or law of economy.

Client: Home MCR
Design: Mark Studio
Design thinking: Less is
more – minimalist use of
image and type communicates
a simple message

31–33
Stockton Road

Home MCR

This brochure for the 31–33 Stockton Road building development was created by Mark Studio for Home MCR and features a minimalist, or KISS, approach to the design problem. The design is kept simple and focuses on the small touches that help make a building a home. For example, a three-panel (double-gatefold) cover features the house numbers that one would find on the doors of the homes. This forms a key visual image in the brochure, and suggests spaces that are lived in rather than a mere building or development.

Gatefold

An extra panel that folds into the central spine of the publication with a parallel fold. Gatefolds present a bigger space to present an image. The example above features a double-gatefold with two extra panels.

Design Thinking Themes of thinking

Python philosophy
Derived from ideas presented by Tim Peters in *The Zen of Python*, these tenets include: beautiful is better than ugly; simple is better than complex; sparse is better than dense; readability counts; practicality beats purity; and refuse the temptation to guess.

White space
Some believe that white space allows key design elements to breathe and be easily seen. It also helps the viewer to focus attention on them, giving them greater impact.

Text minimisation
This tenet suggests that text should be kept to a minimum, with sentences pared back to short, sharp phrases that have a meaningful impact.

Graphic impact
According to many designers, graphics should create a visual impact that grabs the attention and reinforces text communication. However, graphics that go overboard and are too large, complicated or numerous are distracting.

Scale
Designers need to think about scale, an easily forgotten aspect when designing on screen. Design proofing needs to include an actual scale proof for small- or large-scale items such as stamps or posters to ensure that text and graphics are of sufficient scale to be comfortably read.

User-centred design (UCD)
User-centred design (UCD) places the needs, desires and limitations of the user at the centre of every stage of the design process and requires designers to foresee how they are likely to use the resulting product.

Ergonomics
Ergonomics is the practice of designing in accordance with physical human needs, to optimise performance and minimise discomfort. Ergonomics focuses on safety, efficiency, productivity and health in work settings to ensure that products, services and environments are compatible with the human form.

and finally... TIMTOWTDI (pronounced Tim Toady)
This means simply that 'there is more than one way to do it' and follows the belief that a problem may have several different, but equally valid, solutions.

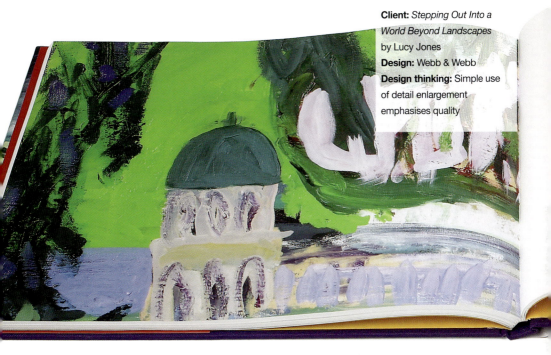

Client: *Stepping Out Into a World Beyond Landscapes* by Lucy Jones
Design: Webb & Webb
Design thinking: Simple use of detail enlargement emphasises quality

Stepping Out Into a World Beyond Landscapes by Lucy Jones

This book reproduces details of Lucy Jones's work at one hundred per cent scale. Using enlarged scale enables the reader to see the brush detail and paint texture, something that is usually lost in the print reproduction of painted works. When paintings are reproduced at a small scale, they tend to lose their detail and look artificial. This presentation allows the quality of the works to be preserved and conveyed.

Design Thinking Themes of thinking

Inspiration and references

Inspiration is essential in any creative activity and design is no exception. Inspiration is key to the generation of exciting design ideas and design professionals draw inspiration from innumerable sources.

Creative people draw inspiration from both obvious and unexpected sources, such as magazines, music, literature and the urban environment. The work of other people in the field, past and contemporary, provides creative stimulation, which is one of the reasons why this series of design books contains so many examples of work by contemporary designers. Designers can cross-reference elements of contemporary life with those of bygone days, and delve back into the rich tradition of art and design history for visual stimulation.

Many designers and design studios formalise the inspiration process to a certain extent though the use of an ideas book. An ideas book is a collection of cuttings, photos, sketches, colour swatches, typographic examples, scribbled ideas, words and found objects that are accumulated to inspire. An ideas book may be a general collection that is continuously added to or it may be made as part of the preparation for a specific project. Designers often create characters that are a mental image of the typical target audience for a design, exemplifying their characteristics, lifestyle, aspirations and consumption habits.

Resolve

To decide, bring to a conclusion or end. A design idea is resolved when it is worked up into a final form.

Resonate

To be received or understood, to come across well. A design resonates when the viewer understands and appreciates the various aspects of the message communicated.

Client: Galvin Bistrot de Luxe
Design: Social Design
Design thinking: Art nouveau-inspired brand identity

GALVIN
Bistrot de Luxe

Design Thinking Inspiration and references

Galvin Bistrot de Luxe

These pieces were created by SocialUK for a brand identity for London bistro, Galvin. They are intended to complement the interior design and menu of the bistro. The pieces reference the art nouveau style from the turn of the twentieth century, transporting the diner to a bygone age of service and luxury. The pieces were prototyped so the client could appreciate how they would appear at actual scale and *in situ*.

Reference points to inspire design come in many forms due to the wealth of cultural information that surrounds us. The latest trends and styles are easily observable on the street, in films, on TV, in magazines and in the shops. Designers also seek inspiration from other creative disciplines such as painting, sculpture, music, architecture, photography and cinema. Designers browse art galleries, museums, libraries, bookshops and junk shops, as well as grafitti-covered streets and supermarkets as they seek inspiration for design.

The visual arts provide a wide and varied palette of historical and contemporary styles, reflecting our ever-changing views of the world. The pursuit of novelty in design means there will always be oscillation between divergence from contemporary styles and convergence towards concepts of the past as ideas get repeated, adapted, built upon, rejected, debased, renovated and tweaked.

The following are intended as pointers to possible sources of inspiration and reference and are far from exhaustive. The rich vocabulary of art and design knowledge can help generate and communicate ideas precisely, and familiarity with such material helps designers expand their vocabulary and be able to draw upon a wider knowledge base to generate ideas, and be better able to say what they mean and mean what they say.

Design Thinking Idea generation

Abstract expressionism

A New York art movement that presented large-scale works containing forms not found in the natural world. Pictured is *Cubi VI* (1963), by the American sculptor David Smith.

Art deco

An elegant decorative style that celebrated the rise of technology and speed via geometric designs and streamlined forms. Pictured is the art deco spire of the Chrysler Building in New York, built 1928–1930.

Art nouveau

A rich ornamental style of decoration, rooted in romanticism and symbolism and characterised by undulating lines and highly stylised natural motifs, as shown on this magazine cover.

Arts and Crafts Movement

A decorative arts, furniture and architecture movement that sought to reverse the demise of beauty at the hands of the Industrial Revolution. Shown here is Artichoke wallpaper (c.1897) by John Henry Dearle for William Morris & Co.

Avant garde

An artistic work that pushes the established limits of what is considered acceptable, often accompanied by revolutionary, cultural or political connotations or ideas. Pictured is *Fountain* (1917) by Marcel Duchamp.

Bauhaus

An approach to design that featured the use of the three basic primary shapes and colours, and geometric fonts to convey a sense of modernity. Pictured is Bayer Universal, by Herbert Bayer, a font based on geometric forms.

Collage/montage

Sticking paper and other media together in unusual ways (collage), or juxtaposing and/or superimposing pictures or designs to form a new image (montage). Pictured is *Das Undbild* (1919) by Kurt Schwitters.

Constructivism

A modern art movement that used industrial materials such as glass and steel to create non-representational objects, with a commitment to total abstraction. Pictured here is a photo montage by Tatlin, 1924.

Cubism

An art movement that rejected the single viewpoint and presented fragmented subjects from different viewpoints simultaneously. Pictured is *Le guitariste* by Pablo Picasso (1910).

Design Thinking Inspiration and references

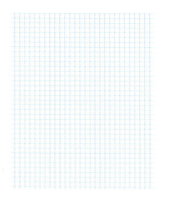

Deconstructivism

A method of critical enquiry that examines how meaning is constructed by challenging the prescribed values that are presented to us. Pictured, the Imperial War Museum, Salford Quays, Manchester, UK.

Grid

A graphic structure used to organise the placement of elements within a design. A baseline grid acts as a positioning guide for text, pictures, diagrams, folios, strap lines, columns and so on.

Kitsch

A style that is considered to be an inferior, tasteless copy of an extant style of art, that may be overly sentimental and/or pretentious, or mass produced items considered trite and crass. Pictured, German Lohengrin legend postcard (c.1900) by an unknown artist.

Modernism

A movement that was shaped by Western industrialisation and urbanisation and favoured simple, utilitarian traits and rejected elaborate decoration. Pictured is Lake Point Tower in Chicago, USA, designed by Schipporeit and Heinrich.

Pointillism

A painting style featuring tiny dots of primary colours that, when viewed from a distance, merge to produce secondary colours. Television screens work on a similar principle. Pictured is a detail of *La Parade* (1889) by Georges Seurat.

Postmodernism

A creative movement that returned to earlier ideas of adornment and decoration as it questioned the notion of a reliable reality by deconstructing authority. Pictured, Jeff Koons's *Puppy* at the Guggenheim Bilbao Museum in Spain.

Design Thinking Idea generation

Psychedelia

A counter culture that challenged traditional boundaries in music, art and design, and saw the use of bright and eclectic colour schemes, interference patterns and curves. Shown here is Brian Exton's *Land of Psychedelic Illuminations*.

Reportage

A style of photography characterised by images that capture and detail defining moments of real life and the joys and horrors of the world. Pictured is Dorothea Lange's *Migrant Mother* from 1936.

Surrealism

A movement that sought to release the potential of the unconscious mind by depicting the real without being constrained by reality. We recognise what we see but it is not as we would expect it to be. Pictured is *La Trahison des Images* (1928–1929) by Magritte.

Tessellation

A repeated geometric design that covers a surface without gaps or overlaps, used in wallpaper design to provide a seamless pattern.

Vernacular

The everyday language through which a group, community or region communicates. Designers can incorporate the vernacular through 'found' items (such as street signs) or slang, for example.

Zeitgeist

The moral and intellectual trends of a given era, the spirit of the age. Fashion, art and design are all subject to the zeitgeist and it is reflected in everything from the height of hemlines to typography.

Design Thinking Inspiration and references

Brainstorming

Brainstorming is a creative group approach to developing ideas and originating solutions during the ideate stage.

Brainstorming seeks to generate many different ideas that are subsequently pared back to a few possibilities for potential development. The brainstorming process starts by defining the problem to be addressed, selecting group participants that will address it, and forming questions with which to stimulate the creative process.

During the brainstorming session, participants have free rein to make suggestions in a non-critical environment. This encourages the presentation of unusual and potentially useful ideas. Resources such as flip charts or a whiteboard may be used to facilitate the process and to record the ideas that are generated. Following the session, ideas are grouped by type and their suitability assessed in order for a shortlist of the best ideas to be formed.

Brainstorming rules
Do not criticise: this is the most important rule. Criticism prevents people from making suggestions and voicing options. Any idea is valid in brainstorming.

Keep the process manager-free: the presence of line managers may inhibit the flow of ideas.

Avoid resolve: do not start working up or resolving an idea that looks like a possible leader during the session. Instead, carry on generating ideas during the allotted time. Ideas can be resolved following the evaluation stage.

Work to a target: a numerical target helps idea generation as participants move away from standard thinking on the subject in order to achieve it. Focus on quantity not quality.

Clock watch: set a time by which the session should end. This helps to keep the pressure on, forcing more ideas to be generated.

Let go: participants must not be afraid of offering odd, wacky or wild ideas, although this does not mean participants should not take the session seriously.

Be inclusive: the session chairperson should prevent any group members from dominating the session and should encourage all members to contribute.

Design Thinking Idea generation

Client: Nokia

Design: Studio Output

Design thinking: Seasonal mailers such as this will require creative thinking – it is important not to discount ideas at the brainstorming stage

Nokia

This mailer was created for mobile phone manufacturer Nokia to publicise its Christmas handset offerings. The brief was to produce a mailer to promote several different handsets, grab press attention and stand out from other seasonal mailers. One can almost imagine the iterative brainstorming process as the design took shape. The design is based around the Christmas carol *The Twelve Days of Christmas* and features a continuous image with each handset paired with a relevant day from the carol and illustrated accordingly.

Design Thinking Brainstorming

Additional brainstorming methods

Brainstorming is the unfettered generation of ideas, but it needs to be employed in a structured way in order to maximise its value and to ensure that useful ideas will be generated. The following steps steer the brainstorming process towards producing ideas that can be developed further.

Visualisation

Quick visual aids can be produced to aid brainstorming and focus attention, although this should not slow the proceedings down or amount to resolve. Visualisation aims to provide feedback with which to stimulate further creativity and build upon suggested ideas and themes.

Groups and voting

The brainstorming participants can be split into smaller groups, each of which is tasked with finding solutions to particular concerns or challenges. For example, one group may address aesthetics while another looks at cost reduction. Groups can vote on which ideas generated by the other groups are to be taken forward.

Scribble, say, slap

Use of sticky notes allows participants to quickly write down their ideas, shout them out, and put them up rather than having to wait for their turn under standard brainstorming. This method also helps people to relax, lowers their inhibitions and allows more timid group members to express their ideas.

Assessment criteria

Finally, to assess the ideas generated requires the need for criteria against which they can be assessed. Criteria can include cost, resources required, necessary resources available, time factors and fitness for purpose. A scoring system can be used for each criterion such as a scale rating (one to five, for example) or a simple yes/no about whether it has been met. This assessment allows the ideas to be ordered and prioritised for follow up and potential resolve.

Design Thinking Idea generation

Scribble
Session participants write their ideas on sticky notes...

Say
...then shout their ideas out...

Slap
...and finally stick their written notes on to the board.

Client: The Deptford Project café
Design: Studio Myerscough
Design thinking: Out-of-the-box thinking for café design

The Deptford Project café

The Deptford Project café is a café bistro and weekend creative industries market in Deptford, UK, designed by Studio Myerscough. The café bistro on Deptford High Street is housed in a 35-tonne 1960s train carriage and features a handpainted exterior and bespoke furniture. This design is an example of out-of-the-box thinking for ideas generation, such as may be produced during a brainstorming session. Without the stimulation of creative thought through a non-judgemental process such as brainstorming, this design solution would never have been conceived.

Design Thinking Brainstorming

Value

Value is a term often used in design. A designer 'adds value' to a brand through the creation of a visual identity, for instance, but what exactly does value mean in the design thinking context?

Value can be thought of in several, quite different, ways. For the owner of a design studio, for example, value is linked with productivity: the work completed in a given time.

Within the context of design thinking, however, we are concerned with the value created by a design for the client. This is more difficult to measure and gauge. Be it a visual identity, an advertisement, packaging or other job, a design can make a highly valuable contribution for the client if it resonates well with the target audience. Design thinking has to focus on producing a design solution that communicates positively with the target audience rather than merely looking different aesthetically.

Designs can add value directly by boosting sales, or, conversely, indirectly by increasing the prestige of a brand or organisation. However, it is difficult to know the real reasons for success as many other variables are involved. For example, is it a new magazine advert that increases sales of a product or is it the selection of the magazines in which it is placed, the frequency with which it is repeated or the presence of other promotions that may be running in conjunction with the advertising campaign?

Testing with focus groups can give an indication of how positively the target group will respond to a design and its perceived value. Surveys can also provide feedback once a new design has been launched and will provide a learning opportunity about the value added by design.

Aesthetic
The appreciation of beauty or good taste, particularly in reference to art, design and style.

Client: Bugatti
Design: Research Studios
Design thinking: Use of top-quality materials for a brochure reflects the product's value, its qualities and its exclusive nature

Bugatti

Pictured are spreads from a catalogue created by Research Studios for the Bugatti Veyron Grand Sport, a luxury car with a luxury car price tag. The design thinking was to create a brochure that reflected the value and qualities of the product, and let readers appreciate the exclusive, prestigious nature of the car. The brochure production qualities are first class – from the glossy art paper stock to the commissioned studio photography and sewn leather cover.

Design Thinking Value

Client: Queen Anne Press
Design: Webb & Webb
Design thinking: Leather jackets with hand-cut illustrations increase collectability and value

Value Equation

William Neal and Stefan Bathe developed the Value Equation to measure value perception. This states that total brand value (or utility) is a function of a product's tangible, deliverable features, its brand equity, and its price. Within the price Value Equation, any of these three factors may be the most important value differentiator under market conditions; where prices are similar, brand equity may govern purchasing behaviour.

Designers add value through creating significance, prestige or other qualities sought by the target audience. The building of prestige through a sense of exclusivity for a premium brand adds value, while emphasising economy adds value to a budget brand. Clothing, perfume and all consumer goods and services are subject to these factors and possibilities. Designers create value by focusing on characteristics of significance: those relevant and meaningful to the target audience; and prestige: high standards and honour achieved through success, influence or wealth.

Queen Anne Press (facing page)

Pictured are jackets for a special edition series of the works of writer Ian Fleming created by Webb & Webb for Queen Anne Press. The jackets are leather and feature hand-cut illustrations. The series is a collector's item with a value over £14,000 (approximately US$23,000). The quality of the jackets, and the design details they contain, add to their value and collectability.

Prestige

Esteem, high-standing or level of respect with which one is regarded by others. Prestige is the value contained in a brand. A car company, such as Bugatti, has a heritage that means its new models are regarded as having a certain prestige.

Significance

The state or quality of being significant. Significance is subjective and refers to how important something is to the individual. For someone who likes luxury cars the prestige of a Bugatti is significant; for someone who does not, it isn't.

Inclusion

Throughout the design process it is important to remember who the target audience is and to consider how design ideas might resonate with this audience. Design must be focused on who it is communicating to and not just the tastes of the designers who create it.

In order to judge how a target group will respond to a design, it is desirable to solicit the opinions of members of that group where possible and include them in the ideate process.

A designer wants to create work that inspires and engages, but ultimately it has to give the viewer a feeling of inclusivity; design is about establishing emotional connections rather than the positioning of type and images.

Inclusion means soliciting the ideas, opinions and views of the target group. Including people from the target group in the design process – perhaps as a focus group – makes them part of the process and gives the group an element of ownership of the ideas generated. This contribution helps ensure an idea resonates with the group, aiding acceptance, and reducing the possibility of arrogance errors by the design team, who may think they know what is best for the target group.

Somerset House (facing page)

Pictured are spreads from a series of books following workshops at the learning centre of Somerset House in London, featuring photography by Xavier Young. The children participating in the workshop were asked to respond to pictures in the gallery: some of the children, for example, were asked to paint a self-portrait in the style of Van Gogh. The book includes the children's drawings and juxtaposes them against the artworks; the three participant schools and children involved are acknowledged on the credits page.

Client: Somerset House
Design: Gavin Ambrose
(photography by Xavier Young)
Design thinking: Inclusion of
content produced by school
children broadens appeal

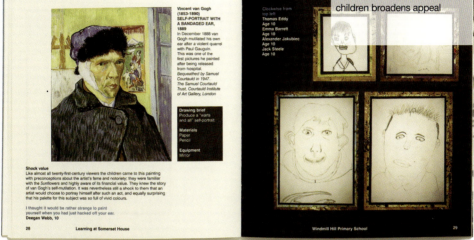

**Vincent van Gogh
(1853-1890)
SELF-PORTRAIT WITH
A BANDAGED EAR,
1889**
In December 1888 van
Gogh mutilated his own
ear after a violent quarrel
with Paul Gauguin.
This was one of the
first pictures he painted
after being released
from hospital.
*Bequeathed by Samuel
Courtauld in 1947.
The Samuel Courtauld
Trust, Courtauld Institute
of Art Gallery, London*

Drawing brief
Produce a "warts
and all" self-portrait.

Materials
Paper
Pencil

Equipment
Mirror

Shock value
Like almost all twenty-first-century viewers the children came to this painting
with preconceptions about the artist's fame and notoriety; they were familiar
with the *Sunflowers* and highly aware of its financial value. They knew the story
of van Gogh's self-mutilation. It was nevertheless still a shock to them that an
artist would choose to portray himself after such an act, and equally surprising
that his palette was so full of vivid colours.

I thought it would be rather strange to paint
yourself when you had just hacked off your ear.
Deegan Webb, 10

28   Learning at Somerset House

Clockwise from
top left
Thomas Eddy
Age 10
Emma Barrett
Age 10
Alexander Jakubiec
Age 10
Jack Steele
Age 10

Windmill Hill Primary School   29

Some of the young artists who took part in the project

Sketching

Most designers sketch in order to quickly put ideas down on paper. As sketching can convey a visual idea for a design or design element very rapidly, it can be used in many parts of the design process, and indeed, throughout it.

Sketching can form part of the definition stage as the brief may be a sketch by the client. It can be used in the research stage as part of the process of creating character profiles. In this instance, a designer may sketch a representation of who the target audience is. This can be broadened into a sketch book that details various aspects of the life of the target audience. A detailed sketch can form the basis of a prototype.

Sketching is perhaps most often associated with the ideation stage, during which a designer rapidly outlines possible design solutions and creates a visual representation of ideas as they are generated. By its nature, sketching implies the rapid outlining of a visual idea and so it should be undertaken in whatever way is quickest and most efficient for the designer. The availability of drawing tablets means that some designers prefer to 'sketch' directly into their computers rather than using traditional materials such as pencil and paper. Sketching digitally in this way means ideas can easily be archived and circulated by email, and they occupy less space than hard copies. However, a designer should use the method that they find quicker and easier.

Digital sketching

A Wacom Tablet, a digital interface that allows a designer to sketch ideas straight into their computer where they can be easily stored and emailed.

Design Thinking Idea generation

Client: Bonfire
Design: Research Studios
Design thinking: Digital sketches rapidly generate different ideas and styles

Bonfire

These digital sketches by Research Studios form ideas for part of a visual identity and typography design for clothing brand Bonfire. These sketches, part of an ongoing design work programme, illustrate how rapidly different ideas and styles can be generated around a given theme.

Macro and micro

Sketching is used as a thinking tool in the design process, for outlining initial ideas at both the macro and micro level. At the macro level, sketching can be used to produce an initial design idea or concept. Sketching can also be used to resolve aspects such as book pagination and roughing out layouts without getting into typographic details and final positioning. As we will show in the next chapter, sketching at the micro level can be used to refine elements of a design prior to the final work-up; for resolving the key details of a logo, for example.

Thumbnail sketching

An example of sketching thumbnails at the macro level, where the idea is to block out the content of different pages. Here the magenta colour denotes one image type (for example atmospheric) while the cyan represents another (for example technical). A sketch of this type allows a designer to think through the pace and flow of a project without becoming bogged down in the detail.

Flowers (facing page)

This book features a typography of sketched letters, which will appear on the dust jacket and the hardbound cover. This treatment reflects the artist's work and conveys a sense of care and craft.

Client: Flowers
Design: Webb & Webb
Design thinking: Sketched typography used on a final design conveys a sense of care and craft

Presenting ideas

Potential design solutions have to be presented to the client, who will then choose one for implementation. Presenting ideas well is crucial; a good idea presented badly can fall at the first hurdle.

The candidate solutions need to be presented in such a way that the client can appreciate and understand the thought processes behind them and the messages they are trying to communicate. Each solution should be presented in the same way, where possible, so as not to introduce any bias towards one particular solution. The design team can state which is its preferred candidate, but the final decision is the client's.

The artwork for the design is typically presented on white boards so that the clients can take them away and think about them. This includes mock-ups at actual scale. This stage may also include a computer presentation using Powerpoint or similar software.

Don't assume

When presenting ideas, it is important not to make assumptions about how the client will assess them or the information they will need to make a decision. The presentation should include all pertinent information, including a clear idea about the scale of the final production. It is important for the design team to practise a presentation in order to ensure that it contains all relevant information.

Checklist:

Is the focus on key information and visuals?

Have bullet points been used for conciseness?

Have key decisions been explained clearly?

Have visuals been printed to a high quality?

Are visuals mounted on boards for clients to handle?

Have you practised your presentation?

Are there any spelling or grammatical errors?

Have terms been used consistently?

Design Thinking Idea generation

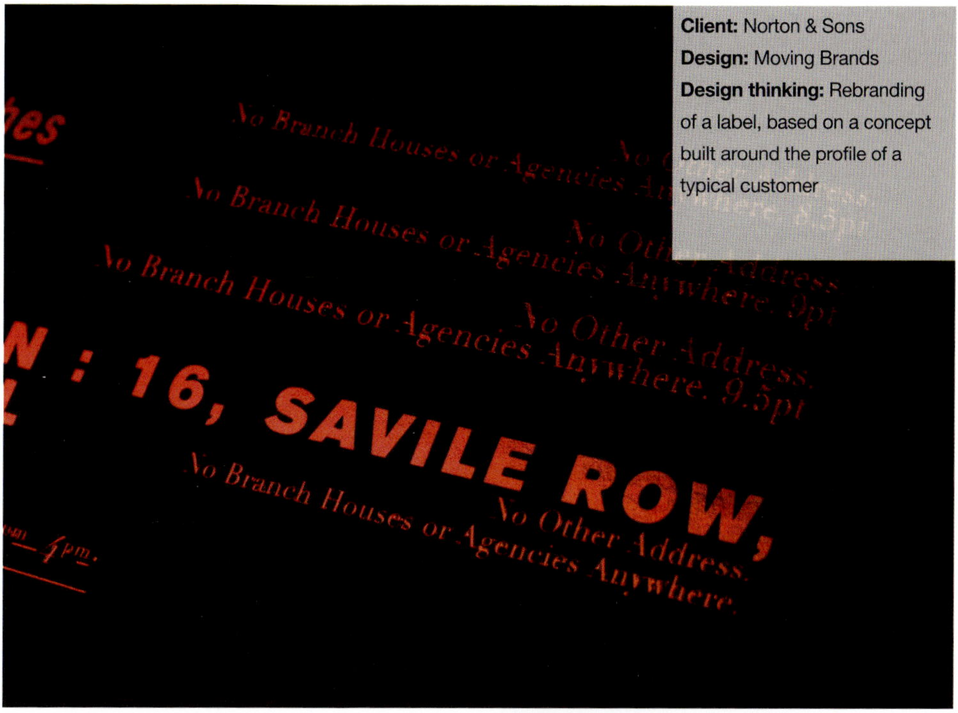

Client: Norton & Sons
Design: Moving Brands
Design thinking: Rebranding of a label, based on a concept built around the profile of a typical customer

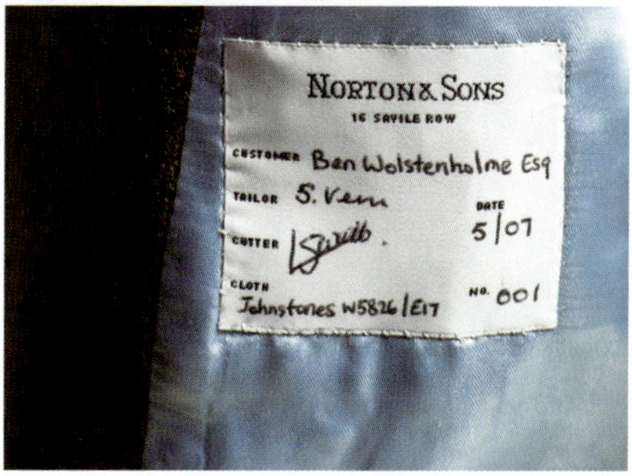

Norton & Sons

The elements shown here are from an identity created by Moving Brands for Savile Row tailor Norton & Sons as part of a rebranding exercise. The identity aims to present the idea of 'the Englishman at large', a concept built around the profile of a typical customer on an imaginary journey, in order to appeal to a dynamic, younger market. This includes references to the finer things in life such as quality tailoring, presented amid a modern, travel-filled life. The identity concept is flexible enough to support brand extension to a wider spectrum of products such as leather goods. The identity was rolled out on stationery and retail material, from compliments slips to suit bags and the shop frontage.

Design Thinking Presenting ideas

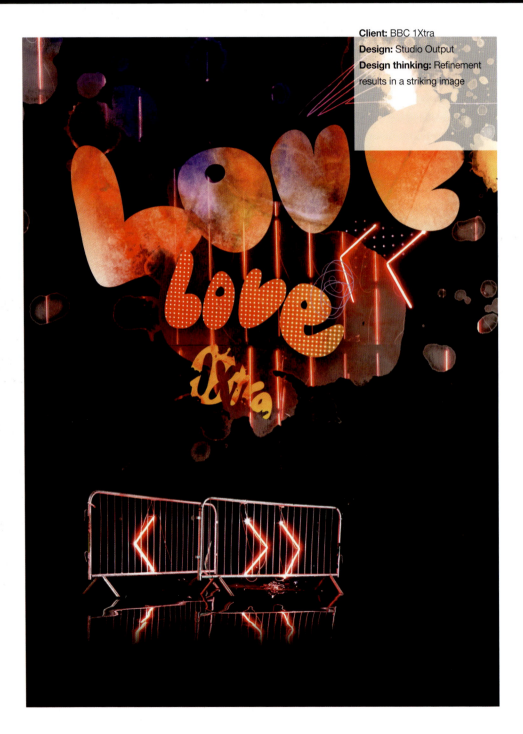

Client: BBC 1Xtra
Design: Studio Output
Design thinking: Refinement results in a striking image

Refinement

Working up a design idea involves the continued refinement of the artwork and the message it communicates. Refinement sees small yet significant changes made to a design in order to enhance the idea and increase the effectiveness of its ability to communicate.

As a designer works up and refines an idea, a variety of typographic choices and images may be tested. These can be resized, recoloured, repositioned, modified and otherwise altered as the designer tries to get the design 'just right'. Refinement may see many iterations of a piece being undertaken before the design has the required tone or emphasis.

A design contains many different facets that come together in the final job. While these are usually addressed simultaneously during a design job, this chapter is split into component parts; images, words, shapes, proportion, numbers and colour will each be examined in isolation. When combined, they create a final design but you can think about each one separately.

BBC 1Xtra (facing page)

This campaign was created for the launch of the digital radio station BBC 1Xtra. As a station dedicated to promoting black music, its campaign needed to keep a broad audience appeal. The result is a stylised image, suggestive of the cultural and emotional qualities that the brand aspires to through its playlist. This is the result of considerable refinement in the selection of the elements within the image: the art direction, the colours and lighting used and the type style, for example. Given the number of decision points, the end result could have been very different.

Thinking in images

Images have the ability to convey an idea or a lot of information very quickly, which is why images are such a prominent part of graphic design. As we all know, a picture paints a thousand words, so it is worth spending adequate time on image selection and presentation.

Images can be used to communicate in many different ways as they are very versatile and their reading can be conditioned by other factors at play during their presentation. Images can have different cultural and social interpretations and these can be shaped by the contexts within which they are used.
The cultural groups they are directed towards, the inclusion or exclusion of particular signs and symbols shared by a cultural group, the use or absence of conditioning agents such as wit and humour and appropriation of historical meaning, are all factors that might influence the meaning drawn from an image. The way an image or design is rendered also has an impact; a black-and-white sketch conveys a different feel from a glossy print, for example.

Receiving and interpreting images
What this means in practice is that one cannot just show a picture of a house. The designer must think about other design aspects that will condition how the viewer receives or interprets the image of the house. Does the house represent an Englishman's castle, a home, an architectural work, a source of joy or sorrow?

Client: Trafalgar Hotel
Design: Social Design
Design thinking: Images representing aspects of hotel services are used as icons to create patterns

In-Room
Menu

Trafalgar Room

Rockwell
Lower

Food & Drink

Upper
Rockwell

Drinks

Upper
Rockwell

Food

Trafalgar Hotel

Pictured are print pieces created by Social for a rebrand of the Trafalgar Hotel in London. The designs feature patterns made up of icons that represent different aspects of the hotel's service. For example, a glass pattern is used for the drinks menu and a balloon whisk for the food menu. Within the context of a retail environment, the use of patterns softens the dining experience and creates a point of interest.

Thinking in signs

A sign is a powerful communication device: it can be easily recognised and can convey complex concepts in a simple fashion. Images can contain different signs. Signs convey meaning through processes of semiotics, denotation and cognition.

Semiotics

Semiotics offers an explanation as to how people extract meaning from words, sounds and pictures. Semiotics proposes that three 'classifiers' exist: the sign, the system and the context. A sign offers information by way of its content, the system is the scheme within which the sign operates (such as a road-signage scheme), and the context is the scheme within which the sign is placed (such as nearby moving machinery). Many designs include symbolic references or signs that communicate multiple layers of information.

Denotation

This refers to the literal and primary meaning of an image or graphic. Denotation means that something is exactly what it appears to be.

Cognition

Understanding, knowing or interpreting based on what has been perceived, learned or reasoned. The cognitive interpretation of an image depends upon how it is presented. Our denotative interpretation of an image changes as the presentation of the image alters. Such changes can be made by context, colouration, juxtaposition or in other ways.

Design Thinking Refinement

Thames & Hudson (facing page)

Volume is a book about Australian architecture firm John Wardle Architects. The pages, which showcase the work of the architectural practice, are styled like a sketchbook and feature sketches, photos, plans and annotations, giving a sense of creativity in progress. This approach also reflects the firm's collaborative studio environment.

Client: Thames & Hudson
Design: 3 Deep Design
Design thinking: Presentation of material in the style of a sketchbook gives a sense of creativity in progress

into being complicit in the inner workin...
And adjacent is his relishing of t...
in the work of his allies in the arts and c...
he admires, collects, and installs.

The third image is from the writings o...
as he describes how inapposite our mind...
is, speculating that our entire body is a qu...
in that every cell within us is composed of t...
tubules lined with nodules that may or ...
a particle in a binary coding system, and th...
in 'heavy water' with molecules aligned in...
every part of our body has a memory capab...
as we once imagined was that of the brain. '...
sider what the 'hand' knows, as much as we ...
what the 'mind' knows. In embracing distrib...
we are in the presence of design thinking, ...
suspends linear logic in favour of holistic cr...
intelligence based on the analogy of 'weak fo...
allows us to make connections in the pur...
to complex, multi-layered problems—as all architectural
problems are—that our usual rationality hides from us.

Wardle describes various strategies that he holds in reserve
to shock his practice out of easy rational linearity into inclusive,
divergent thinking, the kind that chooses the solutions that
open up possibilities rather than closing them down in favour
of one true way.

It is this suspension process that allows a rich body of
architecture to emerge from relatively few strategic moves
within each project. This is not a new phenomenon. It can be
seen in the work of Sir John Soane, whose architecture—
working with a quasi-enlightenment vision of the nature of the
universe—uses the same ploys over and again. Soane's mixing
the virtual establishment of ideal rooms, wrapping of sites with
walls, and a toy-block like articulation of elements to create
a body of work has haunted generations of architects.'

In his Masters study at RMIT, Wardle distinguishes
between two categories of work: over-arching processes
and themes deployed in the seeking of form, spatiality
and materiality. His processes are listed as the diagram and
the act of drawing, 'the use of analogy' and 'stretching time'.

On 'the use of analogy' Wardle cites the Balnarring Beach
House – 'a house that operates like a suitcase ...' At Shibui

Salon, South Yarra (1995) he writes: 'used the hair follicle,
a constant extrusion, cut to length.' At RMIT ICGT
'the symbiotic relationship between the exterior surface
and the interior profiling of (an) aluminium extrusion ...
is of architectural interest.' The enriching detail in the
interlocking junctions of the concrete panels in the side walls
of the ICGT arises as an analogy with both the process
of image registration in printing, and with dovetail jointing
in cabinet making.

These analogies are not whims, he argues. They enable
a design team leader to guide the team towards design resolution. They pepper the work with an almost Pop robustness.
The circulation nodes at RMIT Biosciences Building (1998–
2002) contain suspended 'petri-dishes' that form conversation
pits in the air; the artist clients of the Diamond Bay House
(2001–05) are treated to the vast arch of the National Gallery
of Victoria in Melbourne, as a portal between 'production'
(the studio) and 'exhibition' in the living zone.

On 'stretching design time', Wardle describes how
he also guides design teams through a conscious process
of delayed designing, the powerful graphic gives the teams
the first clues, providing broad organisational principles
and evoking 'imaginative potential'. He avoids early clarity
and resolution, ensuring that the design journey lasts
until building completion. All architects could benefit
from reflecting on this process, because it is the key to the
exceptional breadth and depth of resolution that the practice
achieves in almost its entire output.

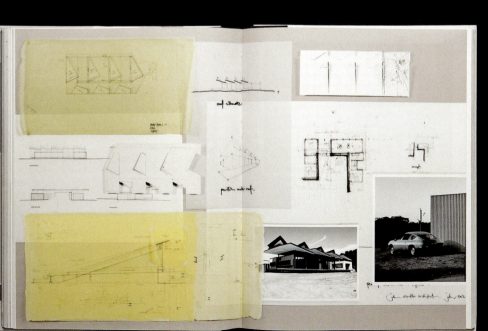

Signs are commonly used to communicate short, important messages in a simple way. As he investigated how people make sense of the world around us, American philosopher Charles Sanders Peirce proposed that signs could be grouped into three categories: icon, index and symbol.

Icon
A graphic element that represents an object, person or something else. An icon can be a photograph and it can be diagrammatic or illustrative. An effective diagrammatic or illustrative icon seeks to reduce the subject to simple and instantly recognisable characteristics, perhaps by applying the laws of parsimony or Ockham's razor, which is to not include too much detail.

Index
An index sign is one where there is a direct link between the sign and the object. For example, most traffic signs are index signs as they represent information that relates to a specific road condition.

Symbols
A pictorial element that communicates a concept, idea or object, but without a logical meaning between them. Letters are symbols that represent the sounds we use to form words. Flags, for example, are symbols that represent different countries, geographic areas or organisations.

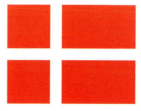

Icon
A graphic element reduced to its most simple characteristics, such as this globe.

Index
A graphic element that has a direct link to an object, such as the presence of old or infirm people, as illustrated in this road sign.

Symbol
A graphic element that communicates a concept such as a state, or country, represented by a flag.

Client: Telegraph magazine
Design: Richard Wilkinson
Design thinking: Displaying images as motifs in a funfair shooting gallery symbolises the endangered status of these species

Telegraph magazine
This issue of *Telegraph magazine* features an article on endangered species. As such, the cover, featuring art direction from Gary Cochran, adopts the motif of a funfair shooting gallery in which the animals are the targets. The use of a target symbol, which is placed on each animal and used in the title typography, underlines this theme and creates a striking image.

Using symbols

The use of symbols and signs in a design requires the designer to think carefully. Symbols communicate effectively because they harness shared cultural norms, which may not migrate comfortably to being used as part of an identity, logotype or branding for a company or product. Certain symbols are universal and may be ineffective in helping to create a visual identity for a particular entity or brand; appropriation may fall victim to the overriding, more generally held interpretation of the symbol.

Symbols can be hugely effective, as testified by the plethora of instantly recognisable global logotypes. In these cases, something unique has been created based on a thorough understanding of a company or product, their history, composition and values. Signs are commonly found in the following:

Logos: A logo is a graphic symbol, designed to represent the character of a company, product, service or other entity, such as the giant panda logo that represents the World Wildlife Fund.

Logotypes: Logotypes function by literally identifying an organisation, using characters styled in such a way as to give an indication of its strengths or culture.

Brands: A brand is a symbol, mark, word or phrase that identifies and differentiates a product, service or organisation from its competitors. Brands are created to help us distinguish between similar product offerings through perceptions of quality and value. The brand then becomes a recognisable symbol for a certain level of quality, which aids our buying decision. Brands often craft a 'personality', which represents a set of values that appeal to their target consumers such as foods that are 'healthier', cosmetics that are 'cleaner' or ketchups that are 'saucier' than their competitors.

Identities: 'Identity' is a term used to describe the behavioural characteristics of a company, such as its level of service and its approach to doing business. Branding is the expression or presence of this identity in the marketplace and can be used to create something unique and recognisable. Companies can employ different identity strategies. A monolithic identity sees all companies or products carry the same brand. An endorsed identity sees a separate brand for each company or product endorsed by the parent company to show the lineage. A branded identity is a fully branded company or product in its own right, without reference to the parent company.

Client: Rootstein Hopkins
Foundation
Design: Moving Brands
Design thinking: Circles
symbolise the positive
influence of financial donations
on the visual arts

Rootstein Hopkins Foundation

Over recent years, the Rootstein Hopkins Foundation has given over £8 million (approximately US$13 million) in awards to art and design colleges in order for students to realise their ambitions. Through their design for an event invitation, Moving Brands was asked to showcase the work of the foundation and tell the story of how a modest sum of money can help to make a positive difference to the visual arts in the UK. The consequent invitation design features circle shapes, a potent symbol representing coinage or money donations. These interact and form connections, representing a strengthening of the visual arts.

Appropriation

When a designer incorporates or annexes an element from another design in a piece of work, this is known as appropriation.

Designers appropriate or incorporate elements from other works in their designs, perhaps drawing on the vast body of work that exists in creative visual disciplines such as fine art, design or advertising. Appropriation is often very direct, enabling a viewer to readily understand the intended message. The capacity for people to recognise appropriations makes it a very effective way to communicate. Some key forms of appropriation are described below and shown in examples on the following pages.

Imitation
Imitation is the copy, reproduction or adaptation of an existing design or image for use in a new design. Imitation provides a short cut to producing an effective design as the design decisions will already have been taken, tried and tested.

Adaptation
Modifying an original design to suit another purpose is known as adaptation. It allows a new design to benefit from original design elements although the content, the message or the medium may be different.

Parody
A design that mocks an original work through the use of humour or satire is a parody. The use of humour often changes or subverts the original meaning.

Paradox
An idea or statement that includes conflicting ideas; paradoxes in design often inject humour or force the viewer to question what they see.

Distortion
An optical phenomenon or deformation of a shape or object. Visual distortion sees the designer change the appearance of an object to make it less recognisable or even to form a different object from it.

Homage
Designers can express their honour or respect for a particular work, artist or genre by incorporating it into, or using it as the basis for, their own work.

Client: Magdalena 2004
Design: Miha Artnak and Ziga Aljaz
Design thinking: Adaptation of a well-known painting to communicate an anti-war message

Magdalena 2004

Pictured is Krik/Scream, an anti-war poster created by Slovenian designers Miha Artnak and Ziga Aljaz, and voted best newcomer winner at the Magdalena International Festival of Creative Communication 2004. The piece is an adaptation of *The Scream*, a painting by Norwegian artist Edvard Munch, that features a ghostly, skull-like head gripped in despair. The adaptation replaces the eyes and nose with the silhouette of an aircraft, while the mouth becomes a dropped bomb. The blood-red flaming sky of the painting has transformed into the flaming body in this anti-war design.

Design Thinking Appropriation

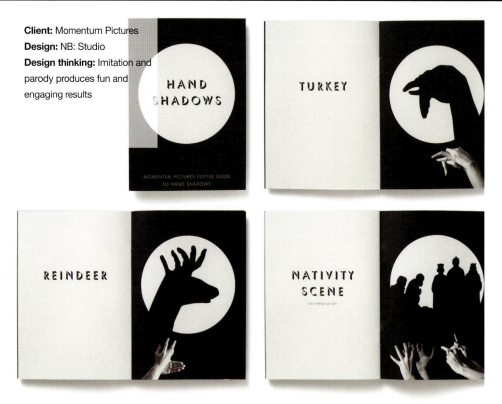

Client: Momentum Pictures
Design: NB: Studio
Design thinking: Imitation and parody produces fun and engaging results

Momentum Pictures

This picture book/Christmas card features imitations of hand shadows or shadowgraphs. The design uses the hand shadows to create silhouettes of Christmas scenes and to create an analogy of black-and-white silent movies. The design adapts the shadowgraphs so that as a viewer progresses through the book, they pass from those that are easy to make up to one that is impossible to do. The result is a fun and engaging Christmas card. Notice the paradox used in the final image to inject humour.

Shaw's (facing page)

This design for a rebrand of Shaw's café in Nottingham, UK, is based on the post-war European feel and decor of the building in which the café is housed. The menus are presented in various sizes and colours, with a simple typographic design. Homage to gastronomes is paid via a quotation from Brillat-Savarin's 1825 gastronomy handbook *Physiologie du Goût.*

THE DISCOVERY OF
A NEW DISH
CONFERS MORE
HAPPINESS
ON HUMANITY,
THAN THE DISCOVERY
OF A NEW STAR.

THE PLEASURE OF
THE TABLE BELONGS
TO ALL AGES,
TO ALL CONDITIONS,
TO ALL COUNTRIES,
AND TO ALL AREAS;
IT MINGLES WITH ALL
OTHER PLEASURES,
AND REMAINS AT LAST
TO CONSOLE US FOR
THEIR DEPARTURE.

A COO...
BE TAUG...
BUT A MAN W...
CAN ROAST,
IS BORN WITH
THE FACULTY

LET HOME
LEAVEN BEFORE
ELEVEN O'CLOCK,
BUT LET BED
BY MIDNIGHT

SHAW'S

LET THE MEAL
PROCEED WITHOUT
UNDUE HASTE,
SINCE DINNER
THE LAST BU...
OF THE...
AND...
GU...

Client: Shaw's
Design: Studio Output
Design thinking: Homage to a well-known gastronome gives focus to the rebranding of a café

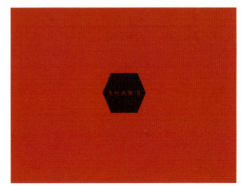

A COOK MAY
BE TAUGHT,
BUT A MAN WHO
CAN ROAST,
IS BORN WITH
THE FACULTY.

SHAW'S

Humour

Designers can create amusing or funny designs to help establish a relationship with the target audience. People have a great capacity to find humour in even the strangest and most unlikely of places, so this can be a very useful tool.

Humour functions by tapping into the shared social and cultural reference points of a group, and what that group considers funny or humorous. Humour functions on different levels – from the *Schadenfreude* joy obtained from watching someone else make a mistake or hurt themselves, to the more subtle mores of wit and irony.

The use of humour can also help to defuse what may be overly serious or stifling subject matter. However, humour is very subjective and what is acceptable humour will vary from group to group.

Rugel (above and facing page)

These posters were created by designer Slavimir Stojanovic at Futro for an advertising campaign promoting opticians Rugel in Ljubljana, Slovenia. Sport requires accurate vision to achieve a high level of performance, and each poster shows, in an exaggerated way, the poor results that poor eyesight achieves. The absurdity of the exaggeration is humorous.

Client: Rugel
Design: Futro
Design thinking:
Exaggeration of misjudgement
creates a humorous advert for
an optician

www.optika-rugel.com

Personification

A design often personifies the particular aims, attributes or characteristics of a company, product or programme into a recognisable graphic device.

Personification is an abstract quality that is used to represent the highlighted characteristics of a company or brand. Designers create graphic devices that personify these qualities so that consumers or customers can form an emotional identification. Many company or brand logos function in this way.

For personification to be successful and credible, the graphic device – and the attributes it represents – needs to successfully resonate with the target audience and be compatible with the characteristics of the product or organisation. If not, it will appear incongruous.

To achieve this requires the use of both top-down and bottom-up approaches to design: top-down in that the characteristics that will be personified must be identified and prioritised and bottom-up in that visual ideas are generated and conceptualised in consideration of what will appeal to the target audience.

Heal's (facing page)

Pictured is a packaging range created by Pentagram for furniture and home products manufacturer, Heal's. The monotone, imageless design personifies the company's simple, clean style, and uses a subtle, dry humour approach to design. Typograms are used as graphic elements to form the stem of a glass, the handle of a fork and the flame of a candle.

Design Thinking Refinement

Typogram
The deliberate use of typography to express an idea visually and through more than just the letters that constitute the word.

Client: Heal's
Design: Pentagram
Design thinking: Typograms add humour to personify contemporary design style

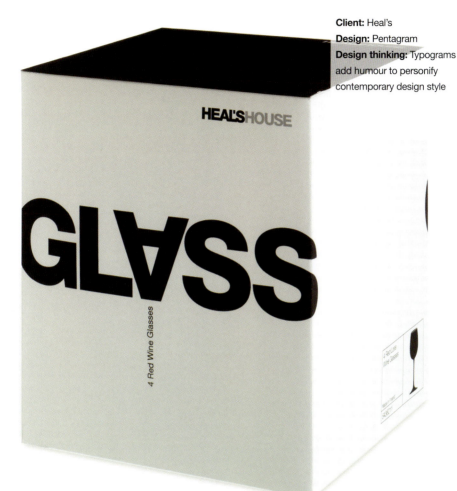

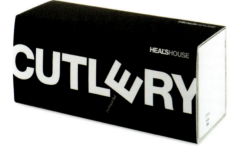

Visual metaphors

A visual metaphor refers to something it typically does not denote in order to imply a similarity to something else.

This new meaning implied by a visual metaphor is often created by the context in which the visual device is present. As such, for a visual metaphor to work (for the viewer to perceive a specific meaning, in other words) requires the presence of shared knowledge or culture. The existence of a common pool of shared knowledge allows the designer to place subjective clues or references within the overall design and this can form the basis of the metaphor.

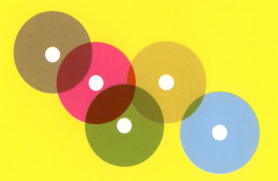

The logo for *Five Towns Make a City* features overlapping circles that provide a visual metaphor for unification.

Medway Renaissance (above and facing page)

Pictured is a large-format book commissioned by Medway Renaissance in England to convey the ideas of Sir Terry Farrell, lead architect and masterplanner of a project tasked with uniting the five Medway towns (Rochester, Chatham, Gillingham, Rainham and Strood). The logo is a visual metaphor for the five towns and their area of influence and the distillation of their separate identities into a single unit. The book was created with five different covers, featuring portrait photography by Xavier Young of people from the five communities. These photographs form metaphors for the towns they represent; the locations in which they were photographed are instantly recognisable to the people from the region.

Design Thinking Refinement

Client: Medway Renaissance
Design: Gavin Ambrose/Urbik
Design thinking: Visual
metaphor for unifying five
towns into a single 'unit'

Modification

Designs often tell a story in a frozen graphic instant. Modification is a key design aspect that transforms text and images in a way that instills them with meaning.

Intervention
By intervening in an image a design can modify its meaning, stress or significance, or change its focus entirely.

Omission
An omission is when something has been left out or forgotten. This can be used to channel the viewer's focus to the omitted element, or draw attention to the context within which the omission occurred.

Opposition
When two or more ideas compete, conflict or resist each other, opposition occurs. In graphic design, opposition is a form of juxtaposition whereby elements are positioned to create an antagonistic relationship between them due to their inherent contrasts – a devil image next to an angel image to represent good and evil, for example. Effective opposition relies on recognisable cultural or societal norms.

Two-in-ones
Graphic devices can communicate two messages at the same time within the context established by the design. This can be achieved by making subtle variations to easily recognisable objects. Their success depends upon the viewer's ability to recognise and interpret the contextual references, which means two-in-ones can be created to resonate with very specific target audiences.

Design Thinking Refinement

Client: Human
Design: Social UK
Design thinking: Modified typography to instill human characteristics

n Visconti

8 5th avenue
rd floor / new york
NY / 10011 / USA

Tel: 212 352 0211
Fax: 212 352 0210
www. humanworldwide.com
Email: morgan@humanworldwide.com

human™

Human

Pictured is a business card, created as part of an identity redesign for music and sound design firm Human, featuring modified typography. An intervention in the counter of the lowercase 'a' has modified it into a sperm shape, whose tail bisects the vertical stroke of the subsequent letter. This sperm character placed in the word 'human' makes a direct reference to the start of every human life and implies that the company has a very human approach to creating sound solutions for its clients.

Design Thinking Modification

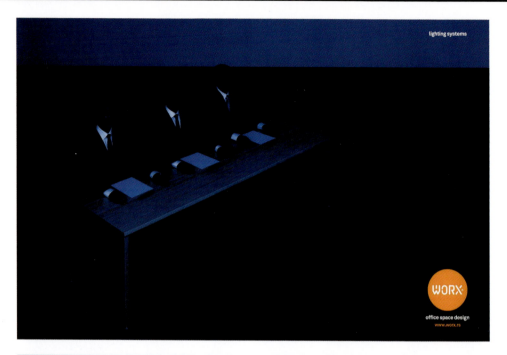

Worx

Pictured is a series of advertisements created for office space design company and architectural studio Worx. Each poster features a particular piece of furniture created by leading Italian manufacturers. The posters use omission of other office paraphernalia to highlight the important role of furniture in our lives. The art direction in this campaign has resulted in highly stylised images that are as slick as those one would expect to see in a fashion campaign.

Client: Worx
Design: Futro
Design thinking: Omission of vital pieces of furniture in the office environment highlights the very importance of it

Client: Ninety Hairdressing
Design: Mark Studio
Design thinking: Two-in-one visual device refers to the service offered and the company name

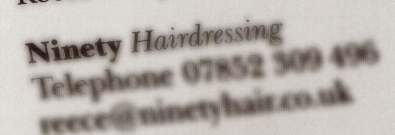

Reece Cooper

Ninety Hairdressing
Telephone 07852 309 696
reece@ninetyhair.co.uk

Client: Magdalena 2004
Design: Miha Artnak
Design thinking: Simple imagery for understated, arresting impact

Tanks a Lot

This poster was created by Slovenian designer Miha Artnak, a finalist at the Magdalena International Festival of Creative Communication 2004. The simple image features the colours of the Iraq flag bleeding and dripping on to the ground, an understated yet arresting commentary on the death, destruction and waste that the US-led invasion of Iraq has produced.

Ninety Hairdressing (facing page)

This design by Mark Studio for Ninety Hairdressing features a two-in-one visual device. The image depicts the eye rings of a pair of hairdressing scissors, making an obvious visual reference to the business of the client. The eye rings and the finger guide also present a visual representation of the name of the company, Ninety,

Thinking in words
Words can be used in many ways to communicate a message: they can help to make it easily understood or can provide a number of different possible meanings.

Designers need to think of words as words but also as visual design elements in their own right, as can be seen in the examples below.

Some words are inherently more interesting than others
From a design point of view, some words are more interesting than others because of the shapes they make on the page, but the inherent meanings words have make some more powerful and arresting than others. For example, 'death' in the example below is arguably more interesting than the word 'bread'.

Some typefaces are more interesting than others
As we will see later in this chapter, the typeface in which a word is set communicates as much as the word itself. Different typefaces have different 'personalities' and convey different meanings accordingly. A typeface can imply classical, futuristic, elegant or streetwise qualities, for example.

And let's not forget, some typefaces are clearer than others
Clarity and legibility are important aspects of text communication. They refer to the ease with which a person can read a message, in terms of the flow of the component words, how the design aids or detracts from the ability to read it, and the ease of reading a particular typeface.

Client: Urbik

Design: Gavin Ambrose

Design thinking: Creation of a new word (neologism) and use of a ligature helps to reinforce the futuristic 'personality' of the brand

urbik

Urbik

Pictured here is a brand identity for Urbik, a brand name devised and intended to suggest, in a memorable way, the company's interest in ideas about the way people might live in the future. This new word 'Urbik' features two distinct phonemes: 'Ur', a coastal city near the mouth of the ancient Euphrates River (now Tell el-Mukayyar in Iraq), believed by many to be one of the first cradles of civilisation; and 'bik', taken from Philip K Dick's 1969 novel *Ubik* about a magical ubiquitous substance and the struggle to find it. Dick's other novels also raise the issue of how we want our habitats to be in terms of architecture, urban design and town planning. Note the ligature of the first two letters, reinforcing the Ur phoneme.

Neologism

A new word, expression or usage, or one devised relatively recently.

Ligature

Two or more letters that combine to form one character. Ligatures are formed to represent specific sounds or words, such as the Æ diphthong ligature, or to improve the visual appearance of certain letter combinations such as the fl and fi combinations.

Design Thinking Thinking in words

Words and language

Messages are communicated not just through simple semantics. Our choice of words and language and the tone with which we deliver them all offer deeper meaning to what we are saying.

Finding a 'voice'

A message can be expressed in many different ways or with a different tone of voice; for example, with authority, with contrition or with optimism. At times we like to feel that someone is in control but at other times we do not like to be told what to do. Finding the right voice is important in order to relate to the target group and not alienate them.

Working with words

The raw material that words represent can be moulded and shaped in many ways and to many ends. The creative use of language can help precisely position an idea, company or product in the minds of the target audience.

The last 50 years have seen a growing acceptance in the media of more relaxed language, with increasing grammatical flexibility and the use of regional dialects, accents and slang. Rephrasing a piece of text into another voice can be done by visualising the kind of person you think would communicate in the required way.

Designers can use synonyms or other related words to move from a formal approach to a more relaxed and tailored one that suits the target audience. This can be done through the use of a table, such as the one shown below, to direct the thought process in the desired direction.

Formal	Reduction	Informal
Company brochure	Us	Our approach
Education buildings	Kids	Learn
Residential developments	People	Live
Masterplanning	Space	Place
Offices	Action	Work

Client: Cartwright Pickard
Architects
Design: Gavin Ambrose/Urbik
Design thinking: Words
selected with reduction
method reflect human values

Cartwright Pickard Architects

These five brochures, one a practice brochure, and the other four each looking at a different sector of activity, form part of a set that introduces Cartwright Pickard Architects as a leading architectural practice. Each brochure cover features a single word, selected to reflect the human aim of architecture rather than the specific disciplines that it comprises. For example, this saw the word 'masterplanning' become 'place', and 'residential developments' become 'live'. The table on the facing page shows the reduction processes that took place to develop the titles.

Vis
Let
cas
to t
and

C

circ
b

Voc
The
spo
as b
Oth
has

b

A
whi

Client: Elk & Wolf
Design: Social Design
Design thinking: Text, imagery and colour palette conveys a sense of style

ELK & WOLF
CHARDONNAY

VENETO

This EXQUISITE *VENETIAN*
CHARDONNAY
HAS BEEN *chilled* DOWN TO
MINUS
NINE DEGREES CENTIGRADE
before cold filtering, creating a
finely textured, velvety soft
& deliciously *SMOOTH WINE.*

13.0% Vol 75cle
Contains Sulphates

Indicazione Geografica Tipica
Veneto 2006
Bottled by Cantine Settesoli, Veneto (Italy)

CHILL FILTERED
VENETO
Indicazione Geografica Tipica
VOLUME 13%   75CL

Design Thinking **Refinement**

Design Thinking **Refinement**

Onc
The
Suff
A wo

Client: Cartwright Pickard Architects
Design: Gavin Ambrose/Urbik
Design thinking: Words selected with reduction method reflect human values

Cartwright Pickard Architects

These five brochures, one a practice brochure, and the other four each looking at a different sector of activity, form part of a set that introduces Cartwright Pickard Architects as a leading architectural practice. Each brochure cover features a single word, selected to reflect the human aim of architecture rather than the specific disciplines that it comprises. For example, this saw the word 'masterplanning' become 'place', and 'residential developments' become 'live'. The table on the facing page shows the reduction processes that took place to develop the titles.

Client: Elk & Wolf
Design: Social Design
Design thinking: Text, imagery and colour palette conveys a sense of style

ELK & WOLF
CHARDONNAY

CHILL FILTERED
VENETO
INDICAZIONE GEOGRAFICA TIPICA
VOLUME 13%   75CL

This EXQUISITE *VENETIAN*
CHARDONNAY
HAS BEEN *chilled* DOWN TO
MINUS
NINE DEGREES CENTIGRADE
before cold filtering, creating a
finely textured, velvety soft
& deliciously SMOOTH WINE.

13.0% Vol 75cle
Contains Sulphates

Indicazione Geografica Tipica
Veneto 2006

Bottled by Cantine Settesoli, Veneto (Italy)

Client: Cartwright Pickard Architects
Design: Gavin Ambrose/Urbik
Design thinking: Words selected with reduction method reflect human values

Cartwright Pickard Architects

These five brochures, one a practice brochure, and the other four each looking at a different sector of activity, form part of a set that introduces Cartwright Pickard Architects as a leading architectural practice. Each brochure cover features a single word, selected to reflect the human aim of architecture rather than the specific disciplines that it comprises. For example, this saw the word 'masterplanning' become 'place', and 'residential developments' become 'live'. The table on the facing page shows the reduction processes that took place to develop the titles.

Design Thinking Words and language

Visual patterns

Letterforms and words have visual patterns created by the typeface, size and case. The visual patterns of letterforms are particularly important when it comes to the design of logotypes and the creation of brands. Notice how the ascenders and descenders alter the topography, or visual landscape, of the words below.

till

Cope has similar shaped circular letterforms – this could be used to the designer's advantage.

Lap's ascender and descender stretch it vertically.

Till appears very upright and straight.

Vocal patterns

The vocal patterns or phonetic sounds and rhythms that words produce when spoken can be replicated to some extent in graphic design. Some words, such as boom, are onomatopoeic; they echo the sound of the thing they describe. Other words have different vocal patterns: bar rolls off the tongue while back has a harsh and abrupt ending.

boom

back

A word with onomatopoeia, which also looks like the noise it makes.

A word ending with an uplift and a trilled 'r' sound that rolls off the tongue.

A word that ends abruptly with a clipped 'k' sound, which can be given a more aggressive delivery.

Onomatopoeia
The formation of words that echo the sound of the thing they denote.
Suffix
A word or stem ending that forms a new word or inflectional ending.

Client: Betster
Design: Studio AS/
Gavin Ambrose
Design thinking: Inventing
a new word for a brand-
naming exercise

betster™

Love sport. Love betting.

Betster

Selecting a brand name that strikes a chord with the target audience can be difficult. For this client, many names were considered initially. These were then reduced via a process of elimination to Betster. Betster is a fabricated word or neologism, formed using the word 'bet' and a user-friendly suffix. The suffix was chosen as it is one that people are familiar with. For example, performance car manufacturer Porsche makes a Boxster car and a betting pundit is a tipster. In this way, the neologism 'betster' sounds as though it is a real word. Having a unique word as a brand name has certain advantages, particularly when it comes to registering a URL for a web address and the ability to take ownership of a particular phrase or word.

Design Thinking Words and language

Puns

A pun is a joke that exploits the different possible meanings of a word or image or the fact that a word or image has different possible meanings.

The pun essentially substitutes one meaning for another within a context, to give an alternative meaning. For a pun to be effective, a certain level of shared knowledge or culture is required in order for the viewer to recognise the alternative meaning. If not, it will appear incongruous and may even look like an error. Polymath author and journalist Arthur Koestler defined a pun as 'two strings of thought tied together by an acoustic knot', or in the case of a visual pun, a visual knot.

The word pun

A play on words using alternative meanings of words and word sounds to form new meanings.

The visual pun

A play on words substituting images for words to form new meanings.

The rebus

Using images to form words based on the nouns they commonly represent.

The word pun
This logo designed by Wolff Olins features a word pun whereby 'Q8' represents the oil-rich country, Kuwait.

The visual pun
This visual pun is Milton Glaser's classic mark that substitutes a heart symbol for the word 'love'.

The rebus
This IBM poster by Paul Rand features a rebus; images that represent the letters of the company's name.

Client: Salomon
Design: Studio Output
Design thinking: A word pun is used to link a company with the familiar saying, 'blood, sweat and tears'

Salomon

This design was created for the bicycle manufacturer Salomon. It features a pun on the phrase 'blood, sweat and tears', which becomes 'mud sweat and gear'. The t-shirt links the core business of the company – making mountain bikes – to the familiar saying.

Design Thinking Words and language

Client: Elk & Wolf
Design: Social Design
Design thinking: Text, imagery and colour palette conveys a sense of style

ELK & WOLF
CHARDONNAY

VENETO
INDICAZIONE GEOGRAFICA TIPICA
VOLUME 13% 75CL

CHILL FILTERED
VENETO
INDICAZIONE GEOGRAFICA TIPICA
VOLUME 13% 75CL

This EXQUISITE *VENETIAN*
CHARDONNAY
HAS BEEN *chilled* DOWN TO
MINUS
NINE DEGREES CENTIGRADE
before cold filtering, creating a
finely textured, velvety soft
& deliciously *SMOOTH WINE.*

13.0% Vol 75cle
Contains Sulphates

Indicazione Geografica Tipica
Veneto 2006

Bottled by Cantine Settesoli, Veneto (Italy)

8 0002534 003064

Design Thinking Refinement

Client: Oliver Spencer
Design: Marque
Design thinking: Geographic coordinates add an eccentric element to a simple design

Oliver Spencer

Email oli@oliverspencer.co.uk

62 Lamb's Conduit Street, London WC1N 3LW

Telephone +44(0)20-7831-6323   Website oliverspencer.co

51.52N,0.12W

51.52N,0.12W

Oliver Spencer

Pictured is a stationery design that features the geographic coordinates for London – 51.52N,0.12W. This code adds an eccentric element to the stationery, referencing fashion designer Oliver Spencer's eclectic collections, travel and sense of adventure.

Elk & Wolf (facing page)

The design of this wine bottle label uses text, imagery and a colour palette to convey a sense of style and coolness. The brand text and image both express the same idea, visually and verbally. Note how they reflect one another through the design treatment given: the animal images are presented as a black silhouette, as is the text, and an elaborate ampersand character in the text is a facsimile of the elk's antlers.

Design Thinking Words and language

Type 'faces'

Typefaces have their own personalities and so it is appropriate to note the different faces or characters they have.

The different roles or functions that type serves within design means that designers need to think about which type personality is appropriate for the message to be communicated. The face that type is set with can help or hinder information transfer, as each face tells a different story, and provokes different feelings within the viewer.

At a basic level, type allows detailed information to be communicated to the viewer. Secondly, as type is a series of marks on a page, it can also be used for a more graphical purpose; the way those marks are formed creates different shapes and use of the space on a page.

Different typefaces have different personalities to the extent that they can be said to actually have 'faces' that tell stories and convey feelings other than the words they present. Some typefaces appear serious, some are upright and conservative, while others are fun, adventurous and youthful, for example.

Type

Bodoni Poster

A modernist serif typeface with a young and sturdy feel.

Type

DIN

A functional and efficient sans serif typeface with a neutral, passive feel.

Desdemona

This art nouveau type has a romantic, spiritual feel that harks back to a chivalrous age.

Cirkulus

A modernist sans serif typeface with a playful, chaotic feel.

Type

Courier

A cold, mechanical serif typeface with a bureaucratic feel.

Brush Script

A fun and animated script typeface that conveys a feeling of youthful energy.

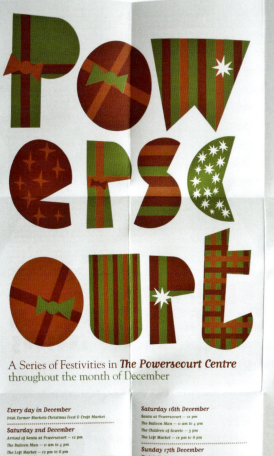

Client: The Powerscourt Centre
Design: Unthink
Design thinking: Text elements set as gifts to give a festive feel to the design

A Series of Festivities in *The Powerscourt Centre* throughout the month of December

Every day in December
Irish Farmers Markets Christmas Food & Craft Market

Saturday 2nd December
Arrival of Santa at Powerscourt — 12 pm
The Balloon Man — 11 am to 4 pm
The Left Market — 12 pm to 6 pm

Sunday 3rd December
The Left Market — 12 pm to 6 pm
Jean Shields — 2 pm to 4 pm
Special Jazz Brunch at Mimo €9.50

Saturday 9th December
Santa at Powerscourt — 12 pm
The Left Market — 12 pm to 6 pm
Mr Punche's Christmas Adventure — 12.30 pm
Dublin Chamber Choir — 3 pm

Sunday 10th December
The Left Market — 12 pm to 6 pm
Nigel Mooney — 2 pm to 4 pm
I'm a Happy Hugglewug — 3.30 pm
Special Jazz Brunch at Mimo €9.50

Saturday 16th December
Santa at Powerscourt — 12 pm
The Balloon Man — 11 am to 4 pm
The Children of Seweto — 3 pm
The Left Market — 12 pm to 6 pm

Sunday 17th December
The Left Market — 12 pm to 6 pm
Jean Shields — 2 pm to 4 pm
Special Jazz Brunch at Mimo €9.50

Wednesday 20th December
St. Andrews Church Choir — 7 pm to 8 pm

Thursday 21st December
Dominican College Sion Hill Choir — 4 pm to 6 pm

Friday 22nd December
Jean Shields — 5 pm

Saturday 23rd December
Santa at Powerscourt — 12 pm
The Left Market — 12 pm to 6 pm
The Children of Seweto — 3 pm
The Balloon Man — 11 am to 4 pm

Christmas Eve Sunday 24th December
Nigel Mooney — 12 pm to 2 pm
Special Jazz Brunch at Mimo €9.50

December Trading Hours
Monday to Saturday 10 am to 6 pm
Late Night Shopping every Thursday till 8 pm

Christmas Week
Sunday	17th December 2006	12 am to 6 pm
Monday	18th December 2006	9 am to 6 pm
Tuesday	19th December 2006	9 am to 6 pm
Wednesday	20th December 2006	9 am to 8 pm
Thursday	21st December 2006	9 am to 8 pm
Friday	22nd December 2006	9 am to 8 pm
Saturday	23rd December 2006	9 am to 6 pm
Sunday	24th December 2006	9 am to 5 pm
Monday	25th December 2006	CLOSED
Tuesday	26th December 2006	CLOSED

The centre will re-open on Wednesday 27th December at 10 am

Visit our Website
www.powerscourtcentre.com

Design Thinking Type 'faces'

The Powerscourt Centre

This poster for The Powerscourt Centre advertises a series of festivals in December. The organisation's name is set in display type with each character appearing to be wrapped up like a present, complete with ribbons and bows. This reflects the fact that the various events are being presented as part of the festive season.

Thinking in shapes

Design elements such as text blocks form approximate shapes on a page. Thinking in shapes helps the designer to address general spatial relationships between the elements.

Thinking in shapes considers the spatial relationships that exist between different design elements and how they fill a page. Various effects can be achieved by thinking of page elements in this way. In 1923, Wassily Kandinsky proposed a universal relationship between the three basic shapes and the three primary colours. He believed the yellow triangle to be the most active and dynamic and the cold and passive blue circle to be the least so.

Harmony
Harmony is an agreement in feeling between the different elements of a design. This can be to such an extent that they support one another to produce an effective and coherent visual statement. Harmony can be achieved on different levels within a design, such as typographic selections that complement each other, colour schemes that are sympathetic and do not clash, and images that communicate the required message well. These varied design elements can harmonise with each other and the entire design can harmonise with what it was created to represent, whether this be a company, product, service or institution. Harmony is pleasing to the eye and is an indicator of good design. As such, it often goes unnoticed, as pointed out in the axiom, 'good design is never recognised, only bad design'.

Balance
Balance is a state of equilibrium in which no single part has a greater weight or presence than another, producing a soothing, peaceful and non-dramatic result. In graphic design one talks of visual balance achieved through the considered positioning of page elements; an even interaction of text, images and white space. In this context, each element can be thought of as a shape that needs to be positioned in harmony with the other shapes within the design.

Dynamic shapes
Wassily Kandinsky believed the yellow triangle to be an active and dynamic form and the blue circle to be cold and passive.

Shape alliteration
Similar shapes can be grouped together to create larger elements. This will help to balance out a page, especially if other large shapes are used in the design.

Drama
The use of more dynamic, angular shapes, such as Kandinsky's triangle, can add drama and interest to a design due to the presence of more acute angles. Each line of text set in a triangular block, for example, would have a different length and would contrast starkly with that set in a typical rectangular block.

Using shapes in design
At a macro level, a design can be infused with different shapes to produce different tensions on the page – different active and passive areas. This will lead the eye to different areas of a layout, and will alter the positive and negative space.

Layouts can also be either symmetrical or asymmetrical. This too will influence shape placement.

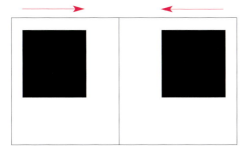

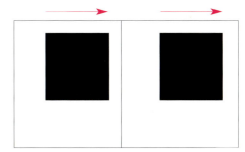

Symmetrical
A symmetrical spread sees the folio structure mirror itself to produce a balanced layout.

Asymmetrical
An asymmetrical spread sees the folio structure repeat to produce a layout weighted to one side. This is more dynamic than a symmetrical layout.

Design Thinking Thinking in shapes

Client: Gas Safe
Design: The Team
Design thinking: An active yellow triangle conveys dependability and avoids confusion for those working with gas

Gas Safe

Pictured are research boards and early design investigations for a rebrand of the UK gas safety body, Gas Safe Register (which replaced the CORGI gas register in April 2009). Investigations around safety signage eventually led to this use of shape and colour, resulting in a logo of high visibility, presence and authority. Note that Bauhaus artists Wassily Kandinsky believed a yellow triangle to be the most dynamic colour/shape combination (see page 121).

Design Thinking Thinking in shapes

Thinking in proportions
The focal point of a design can vary according to where the subject is positioned in the piece and the proportions of the spatial relationships that it contains.

Two basic, yet highly effective ways of dealing with proportions in a design are the rule of thirds and the rule of odds.

Rule of thirds

The rule of thirds is a compositional guide used in design and photography to direct the positioning of key elements. By superimposing a basic three-by-three grid over a page, active 'hotspots' are created where the grid lines intersect.

Locating key visual elements in the active hotspots draws attention to them and gives the design an offset balance that produces dynamic results. With the subject of a design occupying different hotspots, dynamic tensions can be created with the hotspots that are left empty.

Rule of odds

The rule of odds is a compositional guide used in design and photography and places the subject of a design within an even number of surrounding objects, thus giving an odd number of total objects. The supporting objects give balance to the design and help focus the viewer's attention on the main subject.

The focal point of the design can vary according to where the subject is positioned in the piece. This can allow for different degrees of dynamism or energy to be achieved.

Design Thinking Refinement

Client: The Australian Ballet
Design: 3 Deep Design
Design thinking: Proportional shapes create spacious balance

The Australian Ballet

These promotional items, created by 3 Deep Design for The Australian Ballet, feature a spacious balance created by the proportional interplay of the shapes of the design elements (including negative space). The result reflects the grace and movement of ballet.

Design Thinking Thinking in proportions

The golden section

Ancient cultures considered the golden section to represent infallibly beautiful proportions. They observed that the golden section, the approximate 8:13 ratio, was present in nature in forms as diverse as shells and flowers. Due to its harmonious proportions, the golden section appears in many disciplines including art, design and architecture. Its influence on design is widespread as it forms the basis of some paper sizes and its principles can be used as a means of achieving balanced designs.

One simple application is to use the golden section as a ruler that works by measuring out proportions rather than numeric measurements. In this way, the golden section proportions can be easily applied to work on any design – packaging, print or even a website.

13

5   8

The golden section in practice

Pictured above are two examples of how the golden section might be used to obtain proportions in design. The book layout (left) features column widths and image boxes with the 8:13 proportions. The proportions of the bottle (right) and its label are also in accordance with the golden section principle.

8

13

Proportions in art

The rule of thirds is an image composition and layout guide that helps produce dynamic results by superimposing a basic three-by-three grid over a page to create active 'hotspots' where the grid lines intersect. Locating key visual elements on hotspots helps draw attention to them and gives an offset balance to a composition, while introducing proportional spacing that helps establish an aesthetically pleasing balance. Painters have used the rule of thirds for centuries, such as *Portrait of a Woman in Black Leaning on a Grand Piano* by Edoardo Gioja and *The Grand Canal from Palazzo Balbi* by Canaletto, shown here.

13

8

Design Thinking Thinking in proportions

Other numerical methods can also be employed to inform the placement of design elements and so maximise their impact.

Fibonacci numbers

A numerical series whereby each number is the sum of the preceding two numbers in the sequence. Fibonacci numbers are named after the mathematician Fibonacci, or Leonardo of Pisa, who observed this sequence in the proportions of the natural world such as shell growth. Numbers from the Fibonacci sequence are used in art, architecture and design as they provide a ready source of dimensions that produce harmonious proportions. The number sequence is shown below.

1 2 3 5 8   13   21   34   55   89   144

Renard numbers

French army engineer Colonel Charles Renard devised a system of preferred numbers in the 1870s for use with the metric system, initially to simplify the production of airship cables. The Renard system is based on dividing the interval from 1 to 10 into 5, 10, 20, or 40 steps. The most basic Renard series is the R5 series, which consists of five rounded numbers: 1.00, 1.60, 2.50, 4.00 and 6.30. This offers a controlled approach to space division and produces a balanced design while allowing a degree of dynamic randomness as the proportions of the stripes are largely chosen by 'eye'.

10   16   25   40   63   100

Leonardo of Pisa

Mathematician Leonardo of Pisa (1180s–1250) or Leonardo Fibonacci developed a number sequence based on the 8:13 ratio of natural proportions. His findings were published in *Liber Abaci*, a book that helped spread Hindu-Arabic numeral use in Europe.

Charles Renard

A French military engineer, Charles Renard (1847–1905) developed the first dirigible, an airship that could be steered in any direction, in the 1880s. His system of preferred numbers, developed for use with the metric system, was accepted as international standard ISO 3.

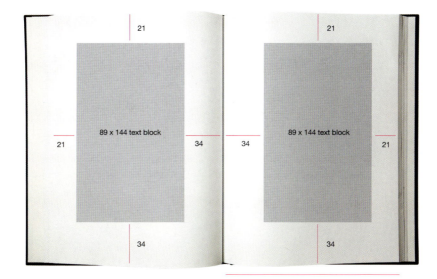

The Fibonacci numbers in practice

A page composition based on dimensions from the Fibonacci series. Using the page width as the starting point, the resulting text block has a proportional relationship to the margins and other design elements.

The Renard numbers in practice

A composition that uses dimensions from the Renard series. This can provide an effective tool for rapidly generating layouts that would otherwise be arduous to achieve. Working in this way can effectively allow you to simply create without having to think.

Design Thinking Thinking in proportions

Thinking in colour

Colour is a powerful communication tool because it can grab the attention and make things stand out and look more attractive. The subtle and sparing use of colour can elevate a design and can apply emphasis just where it is needed to increase the effectiveness of a piece of communication.

The communication power of colour extends much further than simply highlighting particular pieces of text; colours also convey symbolic cultural meanings. The colour lexicon changes as cultures change, providing the designer with an opportunity to better connect with a target group, but it also runs the risk of alienating it, due to colour choices. For example, Western culture associates white with marriage and black with death, but this is not the case in other parts of the world. Understanding cultural colour associations can help ensure the success of a communication, as colour choices can reinforce a message or undermine it.

Blue
Uniform, reliable, safe, traditional, constant.

Pink
Passionate, flamboyant, attention-seeking.

White
Purity, innocence, goodness, clinical.

Black
Magical, dramatic, elegant, sinister, bold.

Green
Natural, foliage, plentiful, luscious, expensive.

Red
Exciting, dynamic, dramatic and aggressive.

Client: Gossard
Design: Studio Output
Design thinking: Bold colours counter the lingerie-pink cliché to shift brand expectations

Gossard

The design of this Spring/Summer 2009 catalogue for lingerie designer, Gossard, uses a flexible grid layout and bold flat colours to provide a contrast to the pink cover. Inside, the clichéd pink colour that is so commonly used in similar lingerie promotions, surprisingly disappears. Meanwhile, the dream-like mood of Jo Metson-Scott's photography helps to shift the expectations of the brand and appeal to the fashion-conscious market.

Design Thinking Thinking in colour

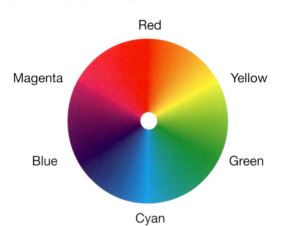

Red
Magenta
Yellow
Blue
Green
Cyan

The colour wheel

The colour wheel can be used by a designer to make colour selections. There are myriad colours available but designers often stick to a limited colour palette that they are familiar with. Designers can use the colour wheel to inform colour scheme selections and try new combinations.

The wheel is the colour spectrum displayed as a circle in order to visually explain colour theory, the scientific body of knowledge about light. The wheel features the subtractive primary colours – cyan, magenta and yellow (these are used in printing); the secondary colours – red, green and blue (produced from any two primary colours used in equal proportions) and the tertiary colours, which have equal mixtures or strengths of a primary colour and the adjacent secondary colour on the colour wheel.

Compatible colour selections

Monochrome: any single colour.
Complementary or contrasting: colours that face each other.
Split complementary colours: two colours adjacent to the complement of the principal colour.
Mutual complements: a triad of equidistant colours and the complementary colour of one of them.
Analogous colours: two colours on either side of a chosen colour (any three consecutive colour segments).
Triad colours: any three equidistant colours.
Near complement: the colour adjacent to the complement of the principal colour.
Double complements: two adjacent colours and their two complements.

Client: E. Tautz
Design: Moving Brands
Design thinking: Use of complementary and split complementary colour selections

E. Tautz

Pictured is a brand identity for E. Tautz, a luxury, ready-to-wear menswear brand that seeks to appeal to an increasingly broad yet discerning customer. E. Tautz, with a history as a military outfitter, is a separate, stand-alone brand from its Savile Row parent Norton & Sons and needed to thrive on its own merit, while expressing the story of 'a wardrobe for a life less ordinary'. Moving Brands created a clean and modern feel by creating a lockup between the monogram and wordmark, expressed in a carefully chosen colour palette of muted natural blacks, greys and copper with a very rich, bright mustard yellow.

Client: Tsunami
Design: Studio AS
Design thinking: Use of prototyping to test ideas for a visual identity

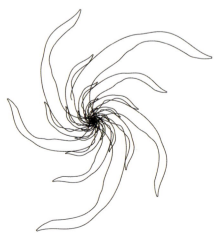

Prototyping

Design is a creative discipline that can generate many solutions to a particular problem or brief. But design thinking does not stop once a workable idea has been generated. An idea or concept needs to be worked up or rendered, so that it can be developed and advanced towards a final result.

A design is the result of a directed thought process that is fed by various cultural, political and factual inputs and so designers test different methods and techniques to develop an idea. Design vocabulary plays a key role during this stage as an original idea is developed, tweaked and expressed in different ways. Different design vocabularies are used to change the accent of the piece, changing the styling from modern to historical, for example, in order to enhance the meaning of a design and improve its ability to communicate effectively.

Once a designer has passed through the initial steps in the design process and arrived at and refined an idea, there is still design thinking to be done. This stage addresses what a design will look like, how it is rendered or crafted. What we have termed 'vocabulary' plays a crucial part here, such as how one expresses something graphically, what its accent is, whether it is modern or old-fashioned, stark or elaborate. This is not about decoration, but how the graphic vocabulary used for a design adds or subtracts, inverts or enhances its meaning.

Prototyping provides an opportunity to test a design idea in various ways to see if it functions in practice and to get a better understanding of how it works as a piece of visual communication.

Tsunami (facing page)

A variety of images that show the development of a visual identity for Japanese restaurant, Tsunami. The images show how visual elements were prototyped, changed and refined as different ideas, colours and shapes were explored by the studio to develop the logo.

Developing designs

The ideation stage will have generated various possible solutions to the brief. But design ideas need to be further developed to have a more precise handle on the message that is to be communicated.

This stage of the design process looks to develop and add flesh to the bones of the concepts generated at the ideation stage in order to facilitate the selection process.

Design and communication strategies need to be thought out and developed to maintain a consistent and coherent line of thought that is repeated and reinforced through all communications. When this does not occur, there is incongruity, which can cause confusion in the viewer, and leads one to doubt or distrust the information received.

Nowhere is message coherence more important than in creating a corporate or brand identity. The identity created has to reflect and reinforce the stated aims and purpose of the company, institution or brand in order to maximise its effectiveness. All organisations seek to differentiate themselves and their products, and this requires an honest appraisal of their nature in order to identify and focus on aspects that can serve such a purpose.

Many companies believe that having international status gives them added credibility: the allure of moving in different markets, having the scale to do so effectively, access to a wealth of local knowledge and support. But how many companies actually are international? Most have a strong base in one country, with perhaps a smaller presence in one or a few others. Even fewer have a presence on different continents. Incorporating an international theme into a message may not be an optimal use of a design.

The project briefing and initial research should have identified the key strengths and direction of the design and it is these that should inform the basis of the message constructed.

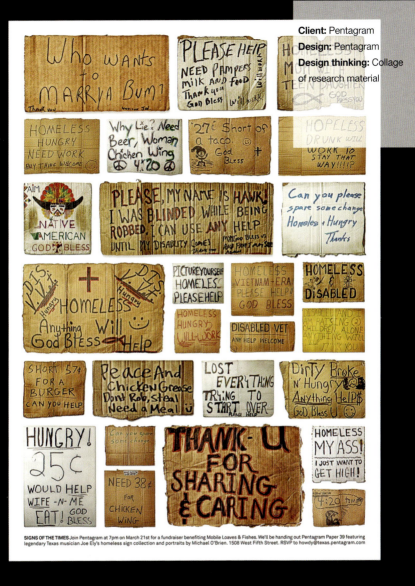

SIGNS OF THE TIMES Join Pentagram at 7pm on March 21st for a fundraiser benefiting Mobile Loaves & Fishes. We'll be handing out Pentagram Paper 39 featuring legendary Texas musician Joe Ely's homeless sign collection and portraits by Michael O'Brien. 1508 West Fifth Street. RSVP to howdy@texas.pentagram.com

Pentagram

This poster advertises a fundraising party for the homeless and celebrates the release of Pentagram Papers 39: *Signs*, a collaboration between Texas musician Joe Ely and photographers Michael O'Brien and Randal Ford, which focuses on homelessness. The poster features a collage of hand-written signs used by homeless people to draw attention to their plight. These were collected over a one-year period and formed part of the the research stage of the design process. As such, the background research forms the substance of the design. It was not worked up further as it speaks powerfully by itself.

Design legs

A design cannot be finite and stationary: it needs to be able to change, adapt, work in different ways and in different settings. A design needs to 'have legs' so that it can go a greater distance than was originally intended. A graphic designer needs to think about this during the design process so that a design idea can evolve.

Adaptability

An adaptable design is one that can be comfortably transferred across different formats, sizes and distribution channels. To be adaptable, a design must be scalable: it must continue to communicate effectively, even if its scale is increased or decreased dramatically.

Stories

A final design should be the starting point for many possible future manifestations and uses and so a designer needs to ask whether a design has a narrative that can be expanded, extended or broadened. A design that does will be easier to adapt in the future to fill a new market segment or reflect changing tastes.

Flexibility

A flexible design is one that can sustain broad appeal across different applications to reach the same target audience in different environments, or that can be used in different settings to reach different target audiences. Instilling flexibility in a design can be achieved by steering clear of controversial concepts and avoiding the use of elements that may date rapidly.

Mrs Massey's (facing page)

In creating a design for food products from Mrs Massey's delicious delectables range, Ziggurat Brands needed to create something that would be transferable across a number of disparate items. The resulting design features a pattern composed of an eclectic mix of kitchen utensils. The design has 'legs' in that in addition to being used on the product packaging, it also can be applied to other promotional items such as the Christmas card (bottom). The design is both interesting and effortless – it does not feel forced or out of context.

Client: Mrs Massey's
Design: Ziggurat Brands
Design thinking: Brand image with 'legs', working across various disparate items

'Types' of prototype
A designer can prototype a job in different ways to test or check different design ideas.

A protoype can also present design ideas to other people, such as the client, so that the concepts involved can be readily understood.

Sketching
Sketching enables a designer to rough out a basic visual idea and the positional aspects of the different design elements. It is a rapid and cheap means of resolving general design issues for a given job.

Model
A replica of a design that allows people to see in three dimensions; a model can have varying degrees of functionality, ranging from simply being a replica of the final shape, to having working components. Models test, respectively, the visual aspects and the functional aspects.

Maquette
A three-dimensional scale replica of a design that allows people to get an overview of it in relation to its setting or location. A maquette brings design drawings to life and is often used in architecture to give an idea of what a building will look like within the context of its location.

Printer's dummy
A printer's dummy is a full-scale mock up of a book, produced using the specified stocks and materials. This tests how well materials work together and gives an indication of the tactile elements of the physical product.

Scale
All prototype methods use scale as an integral part of the testing approach. Maquettes typically use scale to reduce a large design into something that is simpler to digest; models can be actual scale, reduced scale or even enlarged scale in order to give a reliable representation of the design; a printer's dummy is produced full scale; and poster ideas may also be prototyped at full scale to see if they communicate well at a distance.

Design Thinking Prototyping

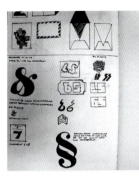

Sketching (above and right)

Sketching forms a valuable aspect of prototyping, allowing ideas to be rapidly tested. These sketches by 3 Deep Design show the development of an identity.

A printer's dummy (below)

A dummy book in the same stock and number of pages, allows a designer to see what it will 'feel' like before printing.

Client: TACH
Design: Innovare Design Limited
Design thinking: Prototyping develops and realistically conveys visual ideas

TACH

These concept sketches show how prototyping can progress visual ideas from the initial conceptual roughs (top left) to more realistic visualisations (bottom left, top right). Created by Innovare Design Limited for jewellery producer TACH (who produce pieces created by gemologist Tatiana Anatolÿ), these prototypes allow the client to see and understand how the final design will look once installed.

Design Thinking 'Types' of prototype

Vocabulary

An important part of design development is establishing the design vocabulary that will enable a piece to communicate effectively.

Design vocabulary refers to the ways in which the elements and styles within a design communicate. For example, the idea of 'freedom' can be presented using a variety of different vocabularies, all of which will alter our understanding of the term. Presented in a psychedelic style reminiscent of the 1960s, 'freedom' would have a different implied meaning than if it were presented in a Soviet-era propaganda style. The following spreads will address some different vocabularies or styles.

Eclecticism
The incorporation of elements from different sources allows a designer to express a diverse array of ideas. In this way, many ideas can be communicated to the viewer: the various sources of inspiration for a piece of work, for example, or a reflection on the content of the product, as in the case of the example shown opposite.

Trompe l'oeil
Trompe l'oeil is an image technique that tricks the eye into seeing something that is not there. Designs can be made to imitate reality through their scale and composition so that from a distance one could be fooled into thinking that an image is real.

Abstraction
Abstraction seeks to remove elements or details of something in order to reduce it to a group of its essential characteristics. The concise way that abstract designs communicate key information may mean they are very efficient. However, their reduced field of visual references may hinder understanding and make them difficult to interpret.

Noise
Noise refers to elements within a design that serve no purpose, such as random lines, dots or odd patterns.

Client: RedActive Media
Design: Richard Wilkinson
Design thinking: Styled like an
anatomical model

RedActive Media

This typographic illustration was created for a feature article in *People Management* magazine, about psychometric profiling and coaching at work. The illustration, with art direction by Carol Rogerson, is styled like a medical anatomical diagram of a head. Combined with this, building blocks are used to represent different mental aspects of the work environment. Some of the blocks have been displaced or moved to communicate the idea that the different mental aspects do not always sit well together.

Design Thinking Vocabulary

Client: SOYA

Design: Frost Design

Design thinking: Youthful vocabulary, displayed via stylised art direction, sharp lines and a muted colour scheme

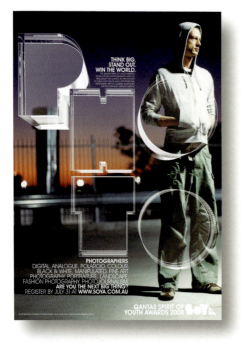

Client: Ministry of Sound
Design: Studio Output
Design thinking: Eclectic artwork represents different music styles

Ministry of Sound
These quarterly posters for the Saturday Sessions at Ministry of Sound feature an eclectic mix of elements in a design based around an audio cassette. Notice how the different designs connect and extend into a much larger image.

SOYA (facing page)
This series of posters was created by Frost Design for SOYA (Spirit Of Youth Awards) and features a youthful vocabulary chosen to appeal to the target audience. This is displayed through the strong art direction, akin to that found in a consumer magazine. This also resulted in a stylised and technology-inspired image with sharp lines and a muted colour scheme.

Design Thinking Vocabulary

Client: GSA

Design: Frost Design

Design thinking: Modernist design vocabulary, displayed through fonts, colours and element positioning

GSA

This brochure, created by Frost Design for GSA, features a modernist design vocabulary in which the grid is used as a device that divides the page into discrete spatial relationships. The modernist styling is maintained through the sans serif font sections, colour palette and positioning of page elements (text bleeding off the page, for example).

Client: Futro

Design: Futro

Design thinking:
Postmodernist vocabulary
adds to dry humour

Never sleep:

a) Alone
b) Tonight
c) Again

Futro
e28

©2007 Futro

Futro

A poster created by and for Futro, which features a postmodern vocabulary,
recognisable by the spartan, unadorned, unelaborated design. Note the dry wit
that the poster presents. The postmodern styling augments the impact of the
subtle humour.

Client: Futro
Design: Futro
Design thinking: Ironic vocabulary constructed by the interplay of image and text

Futro

Pictured are line art illustrations created by and for Futro and exhibited in Belgrade. They feature a strong graphic vocabulary, constructed by the interplay of image and text. The designs convey a deep sense of irony in that the messages contradict what we perceive to be happening in the arresting illustrations.

Line art
A monochromatic image drawn with distinct straight and curved lines, typically against a plain background and without tonal gradations. Before the development of photography and halftones, line art was the standard format for illustrations used in print publications. Using either stippling or hatching, shades of grey could also be simulated.

Irony
When the intended meaning of a phrase is the opposite of its literal meaning.

Client: Cristian Movila
Design: Group94
Design thinking: Minimalist design facilitates reportage vocabulary

Cristian Movila

Pictured is a website created by Group94 for photographer Cristian Movila, featuring a reportage vocabulary. The website remains true to Movila's photographic style and keeps the reportage alive through its presentation of the raw happiness and pain captured in the images. A minimalist design intervention allows the reportage vocabulary to shine. The black background provides strong contrast with the black and white photographic tones, placing the emphasis on the images and making them appear as though they are illuminated on a lightbox. <www.cristianmovila.com>

Thinking Vocabulary

Client: Habitat Dublin
Design: unthink
Design thinking: Brochure implementation encapsulates bespoke idea by using handwriting on the cover

This furniture was made for

me

ON**OFF** | habitat

Once a design has been selected it has to be implemented or produced. This is the stage when the design job is realised, completed and handed over to the client. Implementation is the end of the design process and involves physically putting into effect many of the design decisions previously taken, such as those regarding format, scale, media and use of materials. However, this section is not intended as a guide to production, rather it will provide an overview of the design thinking behind the physical aspects of design that are put into effect during its physical production.

Implementation must ensure that the design the client signed off is produced as expected and with no surprises. It is important to remember that this stage sees the design team hand over the design to other practitioners such as printers, book-binders and programmers. It is paramount that the design team effectively communicate the design thinking to the protagonists of such trades so that the expected results can be achieved.

The design details put into effect during the implementation stage will have arisen during the definition stage, will have been defined and refined during the ideation stage, and possibly trialled and clarified at the prototyping stage. However, as a design passes through the design process, aspects relating to its implementation may have been modified and refined, perhaps due to changes in budget or time scales, format or print run.

Habitat Dublin (facing page)

Unthink was asked by Habitat Dublin to create a flyer to promote a new custom design service. This service allowed customers, if they were unable to see what they required on the shelves, to help design a bespoke product to meet their needs. By doing this, the customer was taking ownership of the product idea. The implementation of the brochure design encapsulates this bespoke idea by using a sticky label image and the handwritten word 'me' on the cover.

Format

Format selection is the first aspect of the implementation stage.

A range of standard formats are available for designers to choose from. ISO paper sizes, for example, are ready and efficient to use and widely available. People are used to using and receiving standard formats in everything from magazines and newspapers to letters and books.

The widespread use of standard formats does not mean that a design is restricted to following the herd. Non-standard and bespoke formats provide ample opportunity to physically differentiate and distinguish a design from its competitors. Producing a tiny book or a large business card, for example, can have striking results.

Non-standard formats offer opportunities for the designer to present information in different ways and this, in turn, provides additional opportunities for information to be communicated to a reader. For example, use of an elongated format for an architectural firm that designs skyscrapers could communicate the idea that it produces tall, thin buildings. A baker could use a format with similar dimensions to a loaf of bread, a builder could use similar dimensions to a brick, and so on. Using different formats can help physically set a company apart from the competition, and this may justify any additional costs involved.

The City Paper (facing page)

Pictured are spreads from *The City Paper*, a monthly English-language newspaper launched in Bogota, Colombia, in April 2008. Inspired by the *Guardian*, the innovative newspaper brought a new concept to Colombia, including the use of a 28 x 38.5cm European format. This format was difficult to implement as Colombia uses US paper sizes, which meant the printer had to trim the stock on two sides. As a consequence, creative cutting and format choices have now become more prominent considerations within Colombian print production.

big picture

Palms from a valley

PHOTO: PIERS CALVERT

It is one of Colombia's most vulnerable national symbols. The 'ceroxylon quindiuense' or Quindio wax palm. Growing in the shadow of the Nevado del Ruiz volcano and the foothills of the central cordillera, it can reach up to 55 meters in height. But its survival is threatened by those who harvest its leaves and bark for the Easter Week celebration. Of the eleven species of 'ceroxylon' growing in the Andes from Venezuela to Bolivia, nine are in Colombia.

First documented in the notes of Spanish botanist José Celestino Mutis in 1785, the palma de cera became a national symbol in 1985 and is protected by law. It can live between 200 and 350 years. In the picture, several palma de cera grow above the cloud forest in the Cocora valley, near Salento, Quindio.

Client: The City Paper
Design: Hugh Avila
Design thinking: Innovative format, inspired by English newspapers, differentiates from the market and requires creative cutting

FREE

the city paper

APRIL 2009 • VOLUME 1 • N° 12 • BOGOTÁ • COLOMBIA • WWW.THECITYPAPERBOGOTA.COM • ISSN 2027-9771

bogotá
In search of beloved books
page 4

feature
From Peru came salvation
page 6

getaways
Chicaque: misty mountain retreat
page 20

THE MINI-MALIST
page 16

Eduardo Martínez is the chef and creator of mini-mal a restaurant with a conscience.

Colombia by Proexport

Of heaven and earth

It is high noon and the horses are under their way through the desert following an ancient footpath crossed by ravines before. In the distance, Villa de Leyva's main square covers almost 14,000 m2, making it one of the largest in the hemisphere and emblematic for its roll-its mark and pastoral green habitat.

Founded in 1572 as a retreat for Spanish clerics and viceroys, Villa de Leyva has been preserved by the passing of time and although it is only three hours from Bogotá by road, it is a world removed from the bustle of the big city. Carved by the cool winds of the Boyacá highlands, Villa de Leyva, is a cascading stream run off life to cover enchantment up the cloister cool evening toes, flowers and grapes. Two wineries operate in the valley producing a young Chardonnay and Sauvignon Blanc. At the Ain Karim estate, one can sample a regal Marqués de Villa de Leyva Gran Reserva and take home a case of fine Colombian wine (www.ainkarim.com). Five centuries have not passed walks and nature trails leading off from the square in every direction.

We head west. Mauricio Cortés, a respected local guide, leads the way on his endless. Surrounded by vast and bearded olive trees we are immersed in a biblical landscape and riding towards one of the most interesting attractions in the La Candelaria desert. El Fósil. Although it can be reached by car from the town in less than twenty minutes, El Fósil or the Fossil, is a place where time stood still 200 million years ago, so there's no need to rush. One must well a morning to visit the remains of the 7 metre long ancient Kronosaurus unearthed in this dried up lake bed by paleontologists back in 1977.

If you go too far to be close with live animals rather than gentlemanly ones, then just off the main Villa de Leyva to Santa Sofía road operates the Esperanza ostrich farm, but the price ad administration can reach a few Ophidios birds, feed them under supervision and milk the painless. It has a restaurant, which serves tender filets of ostrich meat prepared by Brazilian chef Ivan Carvalho.

With several saints honoured, Villa de Leyva and the surrounding countryside, has stable land for business and horticulturalists. Bright worms dart and cold nights are ideal for growing tomatoes, flowers and grapes. Two wineries operate in the valley producing a young Chardonnay and Sauvignon Blanc. At the Ain Karim estate, one can sample a regal Marqués de Villa de Leyva Gran Reserva and take home a case of fine Colombian wine (www.ainkarim.com).

Head to the beautiful 'La Periquera' waterfalls in neighbouring Gachantivá. Here among the raging river and clear cascading falls you can cool yourself off from the dust and the heat of a desert 'oasis'. The nearby scenery is very typical of Boyacá with a patchwork of green, rolling hills and pastoral cottages. For the seventh inclined sportsperson, there are great thrill-and-hang for skydiving. Everchinan Dario Lasso in nearby Santa Sofía organizes special and conveniences with up to 14 descents to be done in groups of six during the day. He also owns an organic bench with hand-picked vegetables and fruit from his orchard.

Villa de Leyva is a place where people and nature converge. The dust hovel of La Candelaria becomes a playground for astronauts and share longest. The skies above 'La Villa' are a canvas for kite fliers and the annual Wind and Kite festival is held in the town every August. And then there are the horses and trails littered with fossils. Don't miss the local mindset market on Saturday with its vendors and local foods. Pick up earthenware pots in picture-sque Raquira and tow the famous Jesquero orange in Sutamarchan.

Celebrating a cornerstone in the earth and the is what makes Villa de Leyva and the region so unique. It's about calm and remembering how grounded we really are to the earth.

To find out about where to stay in Villa de Leyva, restaurants and events click on: www.villadeleyva.net.co or the municipal website: www.villadeleyva-boyaca.gov.co. Colombia Quest organizes outings to the region, www.colombiaquest.com.

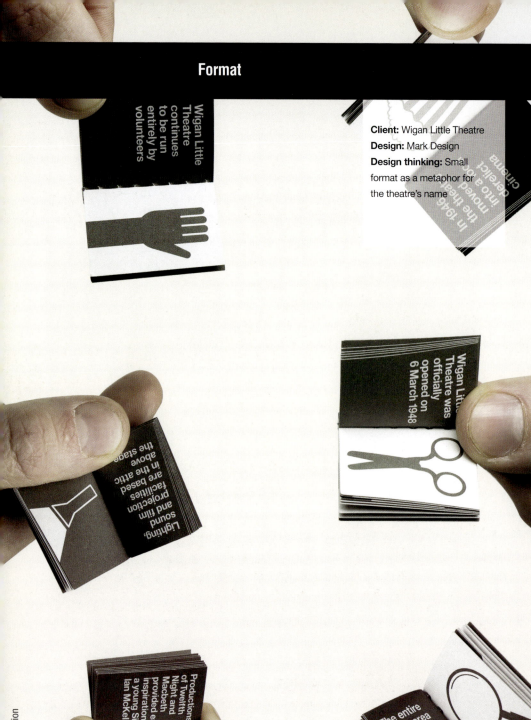

Wigan Little Theatre continues to be run entirely by volunteers

Client: Wigan Little Theatre
Design: Mark Design
Design thinking: Small format as a metaphor for the theatre's name

in 1946 the theatre moved into a old derelict cinema

Wigan Little Theatre was officially opened on 6 March 1948

Lighting, sound and film projection facilities are based in the attic above the stage

Productions of Twelfth Night and Macbeth provided early inspiration for a young Sir Ian McKellen

The entire stage area is only 540 square feet

Client: Part of It
Design: Daniel Eatock
Design thinking: Unusual format to maximise exposure of social messaging

Part of It

Part of It, a charity-driven project, invites designers and artists to create products for causes they feel passionate about. For his contribution, Daniel Eatock chose to highlight the work of the International Dyslexia Association, which focuses on helping individuals with dyslexia and other reading and writing disabilities. The choice of a tote bag as the format means the message can be widely seen whenever it is used, in the street or on a beach, and it also creates a product that can be sold to raise money for the charity.

Wigan Little Theatre (facing page)

The Little Known Facts book was produced for Wigan Little Theatre by Mark Design and features a series of key statements that exemplify the sense of fun and wit of the organisation. The small book format is a metaphor for the theatre's name and also serves to make the information manageable as well as entertaining and engaging.

Design Thinking Format

Materials

The second decision in implementation thinking is to consider the materials that will be used for the production. A wide range of materials and substrates are available that will hold a printed, stamped, engraved, carved, etched, cut or painted image.

With a range of substrates available, there is no reason for a designer to be restricted to using paper stocks. Designs do not have to be produced on paper and extra meaning can be added to a design or message by using something different.

Different materials have different tactile qualities and these can be harnessed by a design and felt by the recipient. Use of alternative materials can add different qualities to a design, perhaps making it more memorable or more of a luxury item. For example, a textile manufacturer could use cloth as a substrate rather than paper. This cloth could then be printed or embroidered. Likewise, a metal producer could use metal that is die cut, laser cut, burnished, printed or stamped.

The use of different materials may also increase the longevity of the design product. It is all too easy to throw away a paper communication, but something produced in acetate, metal or wood may be kept and even displayed.

The design thinking to employ materials at a higher level as part of a design concept typically occurs as part of the ideate stage given that in this instance the material is a fundamental design element. Use of novel materials can, however, also present additional challenges at the implementation stage: higher production costs and different timescales, for example.

Substrate
The material or surface to be printed upon. Substrates include paper, board, ceramic, cloth and metal.

Client: The Art of Chess
Design: Unthink
Design thinking: A woodside stock recreates the feel of a chessboard

The Art of Chess

The Art of Chess exhibition featured work by British artists Damien Hirst and the Chapman Brothers. The invitation to the exhibition, created by Unthink, combines a number of chess-related themes including materials that create the impression of a chessboard. A woodside stock looks and feels like a chessboard veneer, while a solid brown printed on the reverse mimics the felt lining of chessboards. The invitation also features blocky abstract type based on the chessboard grid.

Client: Jefferson Sheard Architects
Design: Peter and Paul
Design thinking: Different model materials provide photographic variation for the client

Jefferson Sheard Architects

This design was created by Peter and Paul for a rebrand of Jefferson Sheard Architects (JSA). Featuring a clever use of materials, the new logo was inspired by the locking shapes of Galt Toys, architectural plans and the desire to create a 3D logo. The design team made three logo models using aluminium, wood and perspex, all of which provided photographic variation and were graphic devices for the client to retain. The final 2D logo is pictured left, whose letters are based on the shapes of the 3D logo pieces.

Jefferson
Sheard
Architects

Design Thinking Implementation

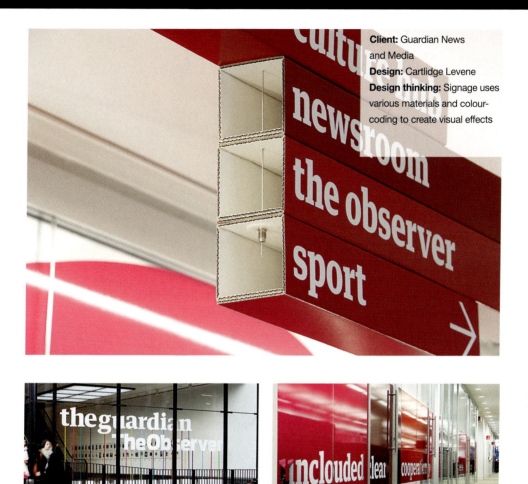

Client: Guardian News and Media
Design: Cartlidge Levene
Design thinking: Signage uses various materials and colour-coding to create visual effects

Guardian News and Media

These photographs show the creative use of materials by Cartlidge Levene for the wayfinding and environmental graphics created for a new visual identity at the new Guardian News and Media offices. Graphic treatments on the glass walls of offices and meeting rooms enliven the open plan floors and feature word pairings from CP Scott's famous 1921 essay, A Hundred Years (written to mark the paper's centenary). Words express 'plurality of opinion' and create a layering effect when sliding doors are opened against the static glazed panels. Materials use for the main entrance sees freestanding 3D letters mounted on poles pushed back and forward to create a visual effect that changes depending on the viewpoint, but perfectly aligned when approaching the building.

Finishing

The materials used to produce a design can be finished in a number of different ways, and this is the third element of implementation thinking.

While this step applies mainly to print finishing, digital design also has finishing aspects, which may include effects such as animations, sounds, introduction screens and delivery mechanisms.

Techniques to consider

Finishing thinking includes the consideration of various print finishing processes including folding, die cutting, foil blocking, varnishing, embossing, debossing among a whole range of other possibilities, such as those identified on the following spread.

The wide range of print finishing techniques available give a designer many options and a lot of flexibility to add elements that help the design attract attention, stand out from other pieces, and communicate a message more effectively or precisely.

Although there are a wide range of finishing techniques available, any that are chosen must be accretive to the aims of the design and must support or enhance the message that is to be communicated. The additional cost that design finishing techniques add to a print job must also be considered and budgeted for at the start of the design process.

Print finishing elements should have been considered during the ideation stage, or possibly during the prototyping stage, but they should never be added on after a design has been selected and printed.

Design Thinking Implementation

D&AD (facing page)

This invitation for the D&AD awards achieves an understated and stylish appearance through the creative use of print finishing, with a black foil block on a matt black stock.

Client: D&AD
Design: Research Studios
Design thinking: Black foil block on a black stock produces an understated and stylish finish

Print finishing techniques

Binding	A process to gather and securely hold the pages of a printed work to form a publication.
Debossing	Stamping a design into a substrate to produce an indented surface.
Deckle edge	The ragged edge of the paper as it comes from the papermaking machine.
Die cutting	Use of a steel die to decoratively cut away stock.
Endpapers	Pages that secure a text block to the cover boards of a case binding.
Foil blocking	Applying a coloured foil to a substrate via a heated die.
Folding	Turning a printed sheet into a more compact form or signature by parallel and vertical folds.
Fore-edge printing	Printing on the fore edge of a publication.
Embossing	Stamping a design into a substrate to produce a raised surface.
Perforation	An area of a substrate weakened with a die cut so it can be detached, or for decorative effect.
Screen printing	A printing method where ink is passed through a screen carrying a design on to a substrate.
Thermography	Raised lettering produced by fusing thermographic powder to a substrate in an oven.
Throw outs	A sheet of paper folded and bound into a publication that opens out to a much larger dimension.
Tipping-in	An insert in a book or magazine that is glued along the binding edge.
Varnishing	A colourless substrate coating to protect and enhance visual appearance.

Corn Exchange Gallery (facing page)

This series of posters was created by Navyblue to promote shows at the Corn Exchange Gallery in London. Note the embossing used on the example bottom right. Also note that they feature a standard layout and typographic house style, which establishes continuity while promoting the diverse subject matter of the exhibitions.

Ryan

Parallax

Private View
Thursday 5th June
6pm - 8.30pm

RSVP
caroline@cornexchangegallery.com
0131 561 7300

**CORN
EXCHANGE
GALLERY**

Constitution Street
Edinburgh EH6 7BS
t +44 (0)131 561 7300
f +44 (0)131 555 0707

www.cornexchangegallery.com

A new home for emerging artists

Florencia
Light Acti
Private Vie
Thursday
6pm - 8.30

RSVP
caroline@cornexchangegallery.com
0131 561 7300

**CORN
EXCHANGE
GALLERY**

Constitution Street
Edinburgh EH6 7BS
t +44 (0)131 561 7300
f +44 (0)131 555 0707

www.cornexchangegallery.com

A new home for emerging artists

Client: Corn Exchange Gallery
Design: Navyblue
Design thinking: Embossing and use of standard layout and typography for continuity in poster series

---

Sue
Spark
Confection

Private View
Thursday 5th October
6pm - 8.30pm

RSVP
caroline@cornexchangegallery.com
0131 561 7300

**CORN
EXCHANGE
GALLERY**

Constitution Street
Edinburgh EH6 7BS
t +44 (0)131 561 7300
f +44 (0)131 555 0707

www.cornexchangegallery.com

A new home for emerging artists

Michael Zansky
Gregory Chatonsky
Michael Rees

Scales

Private View
Thursday 30th October
6pm - 8.30pm

RSVP
caroline@cornexchangegallery.com
0131 561 7300

CORN
EXCHANGE
GALLERY

Constitution Street
Edinburgh EH6 7BS
t +44 (0)131 561 7300
f +44 (0)131 555 0707

www.cornexchangegallery.com

A new home for emerging artists

Design Thinking Finishing

Media

The type of media used to distribute a design will have been identified earlier in the design process but media choice may present different considerations during design implementation.

The advance of technology means that the range of media available – particularly digital media – continues to increase. New media present new possibilities and challenges for design thinking.

The digital age sees a stream of emerging media for designers and their clients to embrace, which goes beyond merely creating a web page. Facebook, Twitter, blogs, mobile phones, Blackberrys and palm pilots require designs to be presented in different ways. The functionality of different media provides the opportunity for designers to extend the functionality of their designs beyond the traditional to include interactive relationships between a design and a user.

The conventions of traditional print media are not always applicable for digital media. This is due to the level of interaction they allow, and the ability for users to choose the content they want to receive and organise.

Designs are increasingly used across a range of traditional and new media, and while certain parameters and functionality may have changed, the need remains for design thinking to achieve consistency in its goal of imparting of a particular message across different platforms.

Design Thinking Implementation

Viral marketing
Marketing techniques that use pre-existing social networks to self-propagate a marketing message. Viral marketing sees the target audience pass a communication to friends and family – perhaps by email, Facebook or Twitter – and typically gives the consumer something for free so that they market other products to create brand name awareness.

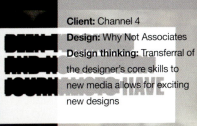

Client: Channel 4

Design: Why Not Associates

Design thinking: Transferral of the designer's core skills to new media allows for exciting new designs

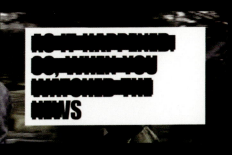

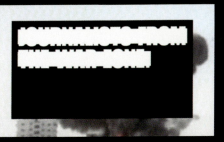

Channel 4

These stills are taken from an animated trailer for a Channel 4 documentary, *Unseen Gaza*. The programme examines the consequences of Israel's decision to ban journalists from entering Gaza during its invasion in early 2009. Design studios are increasingly producing animated titles for trailers, idents and websites as technological change enables the production of such media to become part of their core skill set.

Scale

Implementation thinking also needs to consider scale: challenging preconceived ideas about size can produce a striking solution. Does a book design have to be a certain size, for example?

Design thinking should challenge size assumptions in order to escape the limitations and restraints that their acceptance imposes.

Thinking big
Designers can 'think big' to produce a piece at a scale at which its visual elements have great impact. Thinking big can also mean overcoming mental or conceptual restrictions about how certain topics should be handled or presented, perhaps crossing over into different disciplines.

Thinking big may involve moving boundaries or challenging accepted norms. This sends art into new directions, although commercial success is often used by critics to debase creative achievements.

Thinking small
'Thinking small' is a conscious effort to produce work at a reduced scale to challenge perceptions and offer the unexpected. Thinking small can often appear to be counter-intuitive, as in many aspects of life, people are asked to give more or consider the bigger picture. Thinking small implies the need to engage a more critical eye about content due to the limited space available in small formats.

Outsize
An unusual size, especially a very large one. Outsize formats are often used for books where the focus is on the visual content, such as those showing art works, design, architecture and other visual arts.

Client: Empresas Públicas de Medellín
Design: Cooperativa Mejía Acevedo
Design thinking: Large-scale design to illuminate a large area of a city

Empresas Públicas de Medellín

These installations, from *Lights of Life* by the river Medellín in Medellín, Colombia, form part of the city's 2008 huge Christmas lights display. Sponsored by public services company Empresas Públicas de Medellín, the display illuminated many areas of the city centre as it spread over 27 kilometres of its streets, and included the use of 14 million lightbulbs, 5.8 tonnes of metallic paper, 220 tonnes of iron, 180 rolls of chicken wire and 300 kilometres of hosing.

Inside the image:

Mark Walters
Contracts Manager
Mob. 07971 517 046

West Handley Nursery
Main Road, West Handley
Sheffield S21 5RZ

Tel. 01246 430 784
Fax. 01246 435 231
Email. mark@poplelandscapes.co.uk

popleandshed.co.uk

Pople
Landscapes

Client: Pople Landscapes Ltd
and Shed Grounds
Maintenance Ltd
Design: Peter and Paul
Design thinking: Creative use
of format wittily mirrors
businesses

Commercial Grounds
Maintenance Contractors
Please call for a quote, or email:
peter.botham@shedgrounds.co.uk

West Handley Nursery
Main Road, West Handley
Sheffield S21 5RZ

Tel. 01246 430 784
Fax. 01246 435 231

popleandshed.co.uk

Pople Landscapes

Pictured is a business card created by Peter and Paul for Pople Landscapes Ltd and Shed Grounds Maintenance Ltd. The format features representations of the businesses the cards are for. The Pople side is designed to be like a plant identification tag, while the Shed side looks like a garden shed. This example shows that the small scale of a business card does not mean that a design cannot be interesting, engaging and witty.

Kentish Town Healthcare Centre (facing page)

Pictured is the interior of Kentish Town Healthcare Centre in London created by Studio Myerscough in association with architects Alford Hall Monaghan Morris It features the use of colourful, easy to see, large-scale, medical-themed graphics that fill the cavernous space and provide a reassuring feeling to the people within it.

Client: Kentish Town Healthcare Centre
Design: Studio Myerscough/AHMM
Design thinking: Large-scale graphics fill interior space in a reassuring way

Series/Continuity

The design team needs to consider whether a job is a stand-alone piece or part of a series. Design is seldom undertaken in isolation and a design concept is often rolled out through different media and different items within the same media group.

A visual identity and logo will appear on different stationery elements, on company clothing, on signage, on the website and external communications and so on. If a design will form part of a series, implementation thinking needs to consider how the piece will relate to earlier and subsequent versions or editions.

The presence of continuity can add to the collectability of particular pieces, particularly when they deal with subject matter such as sports, music, films or famous personalities. The implementation thinking can help create value for a piece and can enhance its collectability.

Continuity also manifests itself in the ongoing relationship enjoyed between a design studio and a client. This often results in the creation of many jobs over time, often featuring the same core design, identity or underlying ethos for each separate job. This continuity allows a design team to obtain a deep understanding about the client and the development of a product or brand over a period of time. The design team can then maintain and safeguard the continuity of key elements of a design, from one job to the next, and ensure consistent implementation.

Client: Tate Modern
Design: Cartlidge Levene
Design thinking: Serial element via a two-part catalogue featuring tessellation

Tate Modern

This two-part catalogue documents the installation of a series of five giant playground slides spiralling down into the Turbine Hall at the Tate Modern in London, UK. The first part explores the potential for the use of the slide in the public realm, while part two is a collection of the texts and images that inspired the artist. The two catalogues could be purchased individually, but the cover design suggests an integral relationship between the two by depicting different crops of the same image, tessellated to produce the full image. Depending on how they are tessellated, either the complete image or the titles are readable but never both at the same time. This created interesting display opportunities in the Tate Modern shop.

Design Thinking Series/Continuity

Tessellation
A tiled mosaic pattern created without overlapping or leaving empty spaces.

nursery plan
get ready for
the new arrival

Client: Mothercare
Design: NB: Studio
Design thinking: Naive animal illustrations and standard layout give continuity

the easy way to reserve your
new baby essentials – with flexible
payments and free delivery

mothercare.com

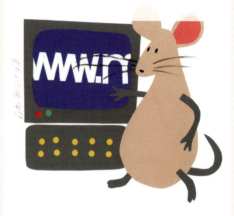

visit our website for 24 hour online
shopping, thousands of products
and loads of great advice

mothercare.com

customer ordering
we'll find what
you're looking for

gift service
finding you the
perfect presents

if it's in stock at our warehouse
we can order it for you
please ask us for more details

mothercare.com

we can help you find the
perfect present – just ask
us about our gift service

mothercare.com

Design Thinking Implementation

Client: GWD Media

Design: Peter and Paul

Design thinking: Personality is brought to each character via staff members but continuity of an overall identity is maintained

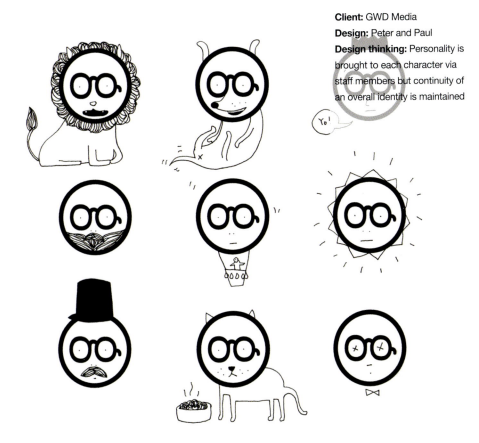

GWD Media

Pictured here is a series of symbols created by Peter and Paul for an identity for technology media firm GWD Media. The identity plays on the idea that technology companies are staffed by geeks. The symbol is a restrained typographic marque based on a 'g' character – the initial of both GWD Media and the word 'geek' – rotating this character exposes the geek inside. Each of the images was created by a GWD Media staff member, thus bringing individual personality to the identity. The result is effective, eye-catching and personal, but the continuity of the overall identity is maintained.

Mothercare (facing page)

Pictured are a series of print materials created by NB Studio for infant product retailer Mothercare. Naive animal illustrations represent key elements of the Mothercare message to new and expecting parents with a simple playfulness that is also sophisticated and witty. The illustrations and a standard layout provide continuity through the series.

Design Thinking Series/Continuity

Glossary

Design thinking is a subject that includes many terms relating to technical or creative concepts. This glossary intends to define some of the most common terms used and associated with design thinking and the various stages of the design process during which it is applied. An understanding of the terms employed in design thinking can help in the articulation of creative ideas. It will reduce misunderstandings between designers, clients and other professionals while commissioning and developing projects.

Design thinking tips

This book has identified the various aspects of design thinking as applied throughout the design process. The glossary contains various general design thinking tips to help stimulate creative thinking to solve a design problem.

1 / Magazines and books

Spend some time flicking through consumer magazines to get rapid exposure to a wealth of contemporary information, styles, ideas, colours and buzz words. Coffee table books provide a window into art and design styles, travel, objects and subject matters that can inspire.

Adaptability
The ability for a design to be used in a variety of different formats, media and locations.

Adaptation
The modification of an original design to suit another purpose.

Appropriation
The incorporation of an element or motif from another design in a piece of work.

Barriers
Rules, laws and other conditions that present obstacles or impediments to the potential success of a design. Barriers include technical standards and the purchasing and distribution power of key competitors.

Brainstorming
A creative group approach to developing ideas and originating solutions during the ideate stage of the design process.

Brand
A symbol, mark, word or phrase that identifies and differentiates a product, service or organisation from its competitors.

Brief
The client's requirements for a design job. The brief contains a specific goal that is to be met by the design.

2 / Objects

Collections of objects, toys and trinkets provide mental stimulation and a ready ability to compare the production, composition and design of a group of similar things.

Character profiles
Written and graphic information that creates a mental model that defines a particular group of people. Character profiles can be augmented with visual clues to construct an image of the life led by a fictional representative member of the group.

Cognition
Understanding, knowing or interpretation based on what has been perceived, learned or reasoned.

Colour wheel
A spectrum formed into a circle, providing a means for selecting complementary colour schemes.

Continuity
The maintenance of specific design traits through different design jobs.

Denotation
The literal and primary meaning of an image or graphic.

Design legs
The ability of a design to be able to evolve, change, adapt, and work in different ways and in different settings.

Design process
Seven steps (define, research, ideate, prototype, select, implement and learn) through which a design job progresses from start to completion.

3 / Swatches

Swatches are produced for special printing ink, paper stocks, fabrics and print finishing techniques. Keep a variety of swatches to hand to see what catches the eye and what is pleasant to the touch. Swatches provide an opportunity to feel the texture and bulk of stocks, and the tactile quality of different print finishing techniques.

Design vocabulary
How design elements and styles communicate through how they look, are presented or dressed.

Design voice
The tone of a visual communication, which determines how it is received and interpreted.

Diagram
A visual device that presents the relationship between different quantitative or qualitative information and ideas. Diagram techniques include Venn diagrams, bar charts, graphs, pie charts and bubble charts.

Distortion
An optical phenomenon or deformation of a shape or object.

Drivers
The knowledge and conditions that initiate and support activities for which a design was created. These include market forces, fashions and trends of the day, and consumer expectations.

Eclecticism
The incorporation of elements from different sources to express a diverse array of ideas linked to the central theme.

4 / Make time for play

Set aside time to load up on different stimuli without it being directed towards any specific project. Read magazines, look at photos, wander the streets or visit a shopping centre to absorb information about what is happening in the world around you.

Feedback
The learning stage of the design process where the client and design agency seek to identify what worked well during the design process and where there is room for improvement.

Fibonacci numbers
A numerical series derived from the observation of natural forms, providing a ready source of dimensions that produce harmonious proportions.

Finishing
Various processes that complete a printed or digital piece.

Flexibility
A design quality that can sustain broad appeal across different applications to reach a target audience in different environments.

Format
Different paper sizes and digital resolutions with which a design can be produced. Paper formats include the ISO paper sizes, while digital formats include screen resolution.

Golden section
The approximate 8:13 ratio that was thought by the ancients to represent infallibly beautiful proportions.

5 / Be disciplined
The design process contains clearly defined steps that channel design thinking. Complete each step sequentially and fully to make efficient use of time, to ensure that nothing is left out and to keep a job moving towards completion.

Homage
Respect or honour shown for a particular work, artist or genre through a design.

Icon
A graphic element that represents an object or person.

Ideate
The creative stage of the design process where potential design solutions are generated using research about the subject to meet the goals of the brief.

Identity
The behavioural characteristics of a company that define the qualities synonymous with its level of service, nature or approach to doing business.

Imitation
The copy, reproduction or adaptation of a design or image seen elsewhere.

Implementation
The point at which a design is produced and put into effect.

Inclusion
Soliciting the ideas, opinions and views of the target group to include in design decisions.

Index
A sign that features a direct link between the sign and the object.

Logo
A graphic symbol designed to represent the character of a company, product or service.

Logotypes
A graphic symbol that identifies the organisation it refers to.

6 / Research
Dedicate sufficient time to research a brief thoroughly. The quality of the research and the understanding obtained from it facilitates the generation of workable design solutions.

Materials
Different substrates that will hold a printed, stamped, engraved, carved, etched, cut or painted image.

Media
Electronic or printed forms that are used to distribute a design.

Neologism
A new word, expression or usage, or one devised relatively recently.

Omission
Something left out or forgotten that channels a viewer's focus by its absence.

Onomatopoeia
Words that echo the sounds that their meaning denotes.

Opposition
When two or more ideas compete, conflict or resist each other, resulting in an antagonistic relationship.

Paradox
An idea or statement that includes conflicting ideas or that contradicts itself.

Parody
The mocking of an original work through the use of humour or satire.

7 / Unleash creativity

The ideation stage is the moment to unleash creativity and so pull out all the stops. Review the information generated during the research stage then follow your instinct when generating ideas for design solutions.

Personification

The abstract representation of particular aims, attributes or characteristics of a company, product or programme in a graphic device that is clearly recognisable by a target group.

Point of difference

The combination of values and attributes that differentiates a company or product from all other similar companies or products. Also called unique selling point (USP).

Proportions

The spatial relationship between elements within a design. Simple guides to establishing design proportions include the rule of thirds and the rule of odds.

Proposition

The general idea and values that a design will present to a target audience.

Prototype

A trial to test the technical or aesthetic feasibility of a design idea.

8 / Springboard

Appropriation is your friend. Become familiar with the designs of competing products or companies. There may be no point reinventing the wheel and so springboard from an existing design and adapt it to your needs.

Qualitative
Information that allows the design team to understand why things are as they are.

Quantitative
Numerical or statistical information that enables a design team to put physical dimensions to a target market, such as total market sales value and annual sales volume.

Refinement
Working up a design idea towards its final form by making subtle changes to design elements such as resizing, recolouring, repositioning and modifying them to obtain the required tone or emphasis.

Renard numbers
A system of preferred numbers that offers a controlled approach to space division to produce a balanced design.

Research
Quantitative and qualitative information related to the subject of a design job that is fed into the idea generation process. Research can originate from primary sources such as consumer surveys or secondary research such as consumer market research reports.

9 / Go leftfield
Unusual or unexpected solutions can really steal a march so push the limits and resist the urge to play it safe.

Resolve
To decide, bring to a conclusion or end a design idea by working it up into a final form.

Rule of odds
A compositional guide used in design that places the subject of a design within an even number of surrounding objects to give balance and help focus viewer attention on the main subject.

Rule of thirds
A compositional guide for positioning key design elements by using a three-by-three grid to create active 'hotspots' where grid lines intersect.

Sample group
A collection of five to ten people who share the characteristics of a target group. A sample group is used to gain a greater understanding via one-to-one interviews, questionnaires and focus groups.

Scale
The physical size of a design.

Selection
The stage of the design process where a proposed design solution is chosen for development because it meets the design brief.

Semiotics
An explanation of how people extract meaning from words, sounds and pictures. Semiotics has three classifiers: the sign, the system and the context.

10 / Disrupt

Deliberately change your routine to do the same task in different ways to produce different outcomes. Put down the computer tablet and pick up a pencil, finger paint, pen and ink or Letraset and put some marks on paper.

Sign
An easily recognised visual device used to communicate short, important messages.

Sketching
A means to quickly outline visual ideas on paper or computer.

Stimulation
The action of agents (stimuli) on our physical or emotional condition.

Surveys
Data collection methods used to obtain quantitative and qualitative information about a sample population: a census, questionnaire, observation or interview, for example.

Symbols
A pictorial element that communicates a concept, idea or object, but without a logical link between them.

11 / Improve your skills

Learn, practise and improve new techniques that will broaden the range of possibilities that you draw your ideas from. Learn to paint watercolours, animate with Flash, bookbind or practise origami. The greater the range of skills you have the wider the range of solutions you will generate.

Target group
A population that shares similar attributes and characteristics. A client will require the design to communicate to a specific target group.

Thinking space
A comfortable and mentally stimulating environment conducive to creative thought with visual, tactile and aural materials that inspire and provide reference.

Thumbnail
An image or page of reduced size that gives a visual reference and allows several pages of images to be viewed at once.

Two-in-ones
Graphic devices that provide two messages at the same time.

Type personality
The character of a typeface, derived from the visual appearance of its letterforms.

Typogram
The deliberate use of typography to visually express an idea through more than just the letters that constitute the word.

Viral marketing
The use of pre-existing social networks to self-propagate a marketing message.

Visual metaphor
A visual device that refers to something it typically does not denote.

Conclusion

This book has outlined the fundamental concepts behind design thinking as practised by designers every day. Different jobs require the use of different thought processes and techniques to develop and work up creative design ideas, with the ultimate aim to present information in the best possible way to communicate ideas effectively to a reader. In addition, design thinking also provides a structure for the design process that helps a designer advance from the ideas generation or concept stage to final production and review.

A thorough understanding of the concepts presented in this book, together with knowledge of the design skills related to typography, format, colour, grids and image, equips the designer with powerful tools to unleash tremendous creativity. Design is a commercial pursuit and the fundamentals in this volume facilitate the efficient use of design time, while keeping costs within budget. Inspiration is the heart of creative activity and we hope that the commercial projects from leading contemporary design studios in this book have inspired you. We would like to give special thanks to everyone who has contributed work to make this book such a visual treat.

Client: Amour
Design: Emotica
Design thinking: Image giving
coherent multiple messages

Amour

Pictured is a logo design for clothing brand Amour. The logo communicates two messages or aspects within one graphic device: the 'm' of 'amour' (which means love in Spanish). The 'm' is sensual (it resembles a heart), but it also conveys a soft, personal feel, suggestive of comfort. All these messages act in a coherent way to reinforce the idea that Amour produces comfy, indulgent clothing.

Design Thinking Conclusion

Client: Studio Output/
Think Tank
Design: Studio Output/
Think Tank
Thinking: Use of a pun to
inject humour into a design

One,
Two,
Tree...

Studio Output and Think Tank.
Graphic design, art direction, campaign design,
press kits, bespoke project management,
promotional packaging, brand development
and print production.

www.studio-output.com
www.thinktankmedia.co.uk

Studio Output™

think TANK
your creative production partner

Acknowledgements

We would like to thank everyone who supported us during the project – the many art directors, designers and creatives who showed great generosity in allowing us to reproduce their work. Special thanks to everyone who hunted for, collated, compiled and rediscovered some of the fascinating work contained in this book. Thanks to Xavier Young for his patience, determination and skill in photographing the work showcased. And a final big thanks to Leafy Robinson, Brian Morris, Caroline Walmsley and all the staff at AVA Publishing who never tired of our requests, enquiries and questions, and supported us throughout.

Studio Output/Think Tank (facing page and above)
Pictured is a Christmas card created by Studio Output for Think Think, featuring a simple play on the words 'One, Two, Three...'. The card included a paper tree that helped complete the pun and clearly establish the intended meaning.

Design Thinking Acknowledgements

Agency	Contact	Page number
3 Deep Design	www.3deep.com.au	87, 125, 141
Cartlidge Levene	www.cartlidgelevene.co.uk	161, 173
Cooperativa Mejía Acevedo	–	169
Daniel Eatock	www.danieleatock.com	157
Emotica	www.emoticaweb.com	15
Faydherbe/de Vringer	www.ben-wout.nl	23, 37
Frost Design	www.frostdesign.com.au	29, 48, 97, 146, 148
Futro	www.futro-icb.com	3, 104–105, 149, 150
Gavin Ambrose	www.gavinambrose.co.uk	7, 13, 75, 101, 109, 111, 113
Group94	www.group94.com	151
Hugh Avila	–	155
Innovare Design Limited	www.innovare-design.com	142–143
Mark Studio	www.markstudio.co.uk	57, 106, 156
Marque	www.marquecreative.com	117
Miha Artnak	www.artnak.net	93, 107
Moving Brands	www.movingbrands.com	47, 81, 91, 133
Navyblue	www.Navyblue.com	51, 165
NB: Studio	www.nbstudio.co.uk	39, 94, 174
Pentagram	www.pentagram.com	99, 137
Peter and Paul	www.peterandpaul.co.uk	160, 170, 175
Research Studios	www.researchstudios.com	21, 71, 77, 163
Richard Wilkinson	www.richard-wilkinson.com	89, 145
Social UK	www.socialuk.com	61, 85, 103, 116
Studio AS	–	13, 113, 134
Studio Myerscough	www.studiomyerscough.co.uk	10, 54, 69, 171
Studio Output	www.studio-output.com	45, 67, 82, 95, 115, 131, 147
The Team	www.theteam.co.uk	19, 25, 30–33, 122–123
unthink	www.unthink.ie	34, 119
Urbik	www.urbik.co.uk	101, 152, 159
UsLot Everywhere	www.usloteverywhere.com	53
Webb & Webb	www.webbandwebb.co.uk	43, 59, 72, 79
Why Not Associates	www.whynotassociates.com	55, 167
Z2 Marketing	www.z2marketing.com	27
Ziggurat Brands	www.zigguratbrands.com	139

Publisher's note

The subject of ethics is not new,
yet its consideration within the applied
visual arts is perhaps not as prevalent
as it might be. Our aim here is to help a
new generation of students, educators
and practitioners find a methodology
for structuring their thoughts and
reflections in this vital area.

AVA Publishing hopes that these
Working with ethics pages provide
a platform for consideration and
a flexible method for incorporating
ethical concerns in the work of
educators, students and professionals.
Our approach consists of four parts:

The **introduction** is intended
to be an accessible snapshot of the
ethical landscape, both in terms of
historical development and current
dominant themes.

The **framework** positions ethical
consideration into four areas and
poses questions about the practical
implications that might occur.
Marking your response to each of
these questions on the scale shown
will allow your reactions to be further
explored by comparison.

The **case study** sets out a real
project and then poses some ethical
questions for further consideration.
This is a focus point for a debate rather
than a critical analysis so there are no
predetermined right or wrong answers.

A selection of **further reading**
for you to consider areas of particular
interest in more detail.

Ethical: awareness/ reflection/ debate

Introduction

Ethics is a complex subject that interlaces the idea of responsibilities to society with a wide range of considerations relevant to the character and happiness of the individual. It concerns virtues of compassion, loyalty and strength, but also of confidence, imagination, humour and optimism. As introduced in ancient Greek philosophy, the fundamental ethical question is *what should I do?* How we might pursue a 'good' life not only raises moral concerns about the effects of our actions on others, but also personal concerns about our own integrity.

In modern times the most important and controversial questions in ethics have been the moral ones. With growing populations and improvements in mobility and communications, it is not surprising that considerations about how to structure our lives together on the planet should come to the forefront. For visual artists and communicators it should be no surprise that these considerations will enter into the creative process.

Some ethical considerations are already enshrined in government laws and regulations or in professional codes of conduct. For example, plagiarism and breaches of confidentiality can be punishable offences. Legislation in various nations makes it unlawful to exclude people with disabilities from accessing information or spaces. The trade of ivory as a material has been banned in many countries. In these cases, a clear line has been drawn under what is unacceptable.

But most ethical matters remain open to debate, among experts and lay-people alike, and in the end we have to make our own choices on the basis of our own guiding principles or values. Is it more ethical to work for a charity than for a commercial company? Is it unethical to create something that others find ugly or offensive?

Specific questions such as these may lead to other questions that are more abstract. For example, is it only effects on humans (and what they care about) that are important, or might effects on the natural world require attention too?

Is promoting ethical consequences justified even when it requires ethical sacrifices along the way? Must there be a single unifying theory of ethics (such as the Utilitarian thesis that the right course of action is always the one that leads to the greatest happiness of the greatest number), or might there always be many different ethical values that pull a person in various directions?

As we enter into ethical debate and engage with these dilemmas on a personal and professional level, we may change our views or change our view of others. The real test though is whether, as we reflect on these matters, we change the way we act as well as the way we think. Socrates, the 'father' of philosophy, proposed that people will naturally do 'good' if they know what is right. But this point might only lead us to yet another question: *how do we know what is right?*

Working with ethics

You
What are your ethical beliefs?

Central to everything you do will be your attitude to people and issues around you. For some people their ethics are an active part of the decisions they make everyday as a consumer, a voter or a working professional. Others may think about ethics very little and yet this does not automatically make them unethical. Personal beliefs, lifestyle, politics, nationality, religion, gender, class or education can all influence your ethical viewpoint.

Using the scale, where would you place yourself? What do you take into account to make your decision? Compare results with your friends or colleagues.

Your client
What are your terms?

Working relationships are central to whether ethics can be embedded into a project and your conduct on a day-to-day basis is a demonstration of your professional ethics. The decision with the biggest impact is whom you choose to work with in the first place. Cigarette companies or arms traders are often-cited examples when talking about where a line might be drawn, but rarely are real situations so extreme. At what point might you turn down a project on ethical grounds and how much does the reality of having to earn a living affect your ability to choose?

Using the scale, where would you place a project? How does this compare to your personal ethical level?

01 02 03 04 05 06 07 08 09 10

01 02 03 04 05 06 07 08 09 10